FEAR IN OUR HEARTS

NORTH AMERICAN RELIGIONS

Series Editors: Tracy Fessenden (Arizona State University), Laura Levitt (Temple University), and David Harrington Watt (Haverford College).

Since its inception, the North American Religions book series has steadily disseminated gracefully written, pathbreaking explorations of religion in North America. Books in the series move among the discourses of ethnographic, textual, and historical analysis and across a range of topics, including sound, story, food, nature, healing, crime, and pilgrimage. In so doing they bring religion into view as a style and form of belonging, a set of tools for living with and in relations of power, a mode of cultural production and reproduction, and a vast repertory of the imagination. Whatever their focus, books in the series remain attentive to the shifting and contingent ways in which religious phenomena are named, organized, and contested. They bring fluency in the best of contemporary theoretical and historical scholarship to bear on the study of religion in North America. The series focuses primarily, but not exclusively, on religion in the United States in the twentieth and twenty-first centuries.

Books in the series:

Fear in Our Hearts

What Islamophobia Tells Us about America

Caleb Iyer Elfenbein

NEW YORK UNIVERSITY PRESS

New York

NEW YORK UNIVERSITY PRESS
New York
www.nyupress.org

References to Internet websites (URLs) were accurate at the time of writing. Neither the author nor New York University Press is responsible for URLs that may have expired or changed since the manuscript was prepared.

Library of Congress Cataloging-in-Publication Data
Names: Elfenbein, Caleb Iyer, author.
Title: Fear in our hearts : what Islamophobia tells us about America / Caleb Iyer Elfenbein.
Description: New York : New York University Press, 2021. | Series: North American religions | Includes bibliographical references and index.
Identifiers: LCCN 2020015032 (print) | LCCN 2020015033 (ebook) | ISBN 9781479804580 (cloth) | ISBN 9781479820528 (paperback) | ISBN 9781479804610 (ebook) | ISBN 9781479804627 (ebook)
Subjects: LCSH: Islamophobia—United States—History—21st century. | Muslims—United States—Social conditions—21st century. | Hate crimes—United States—History—21st century.
Classification: LCC E184.M88 E44 2021 (print) | LCC E184.M88 (ebook) | DDC 305.6/970973--dc23
LC record available at https://lccn.loc.gov/2020015032

LC ebook record available at https://lccn.loc.gov/2020015033New York University Press books are printed on acid-free paper, and their binding materials are chosen for strength and durability. We strive to use environmentally responsible suppliers and materials to the greatest extent possible in publishing our books.

Manufactured in the United States of America

10 9 8 7 6 5 4 3 2

Also available as an ebook

CONTENTS

PREFACE

I'm Not Muslim. So Why Am I Writing This Book?

For the last twenty years, I've devoted my professional life to studying, teaching, and writing about Islamic traditions and the histories of Muslim communities.

I've studied Arabic and spent time in the Middle East.

I've taught courses about the modern history of the Middle East, about the debates that have animated life in the region during the modern period—debates about religion in public life, gender and sexuality, the nature of national identity, and the relationship of societies in the region with Western powers, including the United States.

I've also taught courses about Islamic devotional traditions. I've explored with my students how Muslims have read and experienced the Qur'an in different times and places, and how Muslims in different times and places have understood what it means to live a good life and be a good person.

I've written about debates in Muslim societies about what people need to thrive as human beings—and whether the government should be involved in providing those things.

Throughout, I've learned that one of the most meaningful things about studying communities of people in different times and places is what we can learn about ourselves in the process. The debates that I describe above aren't necessarily particular to Muslim communities in the Middle East or elsewhere. Some of the details may be, but the debates themselves are not. Societies around the world, including the United States, grapple with where religion fits in public life; struggle with questions of national identity, especially in times of great change; and wrestle with disagreements about gender roles and sexuality.

People around the world think about what it means to live a good life and be a good person. Learning how people different from ourselves think about these kinds of questions can be incredibly illuminating about our own communities, our own societies, our own journeys through life. Let me give you an example from my own personal experience.

I was once invited by a local church to talk about Islam. I decided that I would describe how, as a non-Muslim, studying Islam has left a mark on my own life. In the talk I described what I find to be a really beautiful idea in Islamic devotional traditions: that God is closer to us than our own jugular.

I understand this idea to mean that God is always with us, is part of us. God is an ever-present witness to what we do, what we think, how we approach living with others in the world. God is, in other words, the ultimate conscience. This conscience doesn't expect perfection (thank goodness). This conscience expects that at the end of our lives we can rest knowing that we've done more good than harm in the world. I find that a realistic standard, and I've taken it as my own in many important respects.

I don't think this requires that I become Muslim myself. I'm not even sure that it requires a firmly held belief in God. I've translated the idea of God-as-conscience into something that makes sense to me—that reflecting on what I do and why I do it is an essential ingredient of being a good person.

For some reason, the way that this idea comes through in Islamic devotional traditions really made sense to me in a way that Jewish and Christian version of ideas never really did (despite all the time I spent in synagogue and Catholic mass growing up, which is perhaps its own story!). Studying Islam, and the ways that different Muslim communities have brought Islam to life, has helped me learn about myself and my own communities in meaningful ways.

Studying Islam has enriched my life by helping me think about what it means to live a good life and be a good person. Studying Islam has also made my professional life possible. I love teaching and sharing what I've learned with others. None of this—the personal growth and professional fulfillment—would be possible without untold, everyday Muslims past and present striving to understand what it means to do more good than bad in the world.

Over time, I've come to see that I owe quite a debt to the people whose lives have made my own personal growth and professional life possible. When I began to notice more and more reports about anti-Muslim activity across the United States in 2015, I decided that it was time to try to acknowledge that debt and, in some small way, begin to pay it back. That is how this project began.

Since then, I have spent a lot of time learning about anti-Muslim sentiment and activity in the United States—where it comes from, how it's shown itself in different times, and how it became a big part of our public life today. This work left me with lots of questions about the state of public life in our country.

Sharing What I've Learned—and How I've Learned It

The book you're reading now is my attempt to share with you some of what I've learned in search of answers. It's one of my main hopes that reading this book will offer an opportunity for you to learn about a significant part of Muslim experiences in the United States and, at the same time, to reflect on where we find ourselves as a country today. Anti-Muslim activity tells us as much about the state of core American values in general as it does about the particular experiences of American Muslims.

Fear plays a big role in this book. Fear is a significant part of our public life in general, and fear of Muslims has become more and more common over the past twenty years. It's worth considering whether we're better off as a country for letting fear of Muslims contribute to the normalization of what I call "public hate." The experiences of vulnerable people in our midst are a very good measure of where we are as a society in relation to our stated core values of equality.

If you are reading this book and you are Muslim, I hope that it helps you to feel seen by allies and to know that your experiences matter to people who aren't Muslim.

* * *

Before we get much further, I'd like to tell you just a little bit about the sources I use and the decisions I made about that data that we will discuss throughout this book.

Like anyone who has questions, I started out just trying to find whatever was already out there that could help me answer them. In my case that meant reading work being done by scholars and journalists on Muslim experiences in the United States. I did have a head start on the search because back in 2011 I had put together a course at Grinnell College called Being Muslim in America. Coming just after a big controversy in late 2010 involving a proposed mosque and community center in lower Manhattan, I had wanted to learn more about people's experiences of being Muslim in the United States from the country's beginning through today. The reading I did back then provided me with an excellent foundation for a renewed exploration in 2015.

I quickly realized that lots more people had been writing on this subject since I had first started looking years earlier. I build upon the work of other people throughout this book.[1]

As I continued my research, I also began reading as many news reports about anti-Muslim activity as I could get my hands on. I wanted to learn about what Muslims across the country were experiencing in their lives as anti-Muslim sentiment seemed to be growing into a larger presence in public life. Soon, I had students working with me collecting articles. We began adding each news report to a dataset of anti-Muslim incidents, which we used to start a website called Mapping Islamophobia.[2] This original dataset, the first of its kind, has over fifteen hundred news reports and allows us to identify trends in anti-Muslim activity. I've learned so much from reading all of these articles.

I've tried to be very careful about the sources I've used. My general rule has been to use information from newspapers that have a clear editorial policy and chain of command. Whenever possible I use articles from local newspapers. I want to be sure that you, as my reader, can trust the information I'm giving you.[3] Establishing that trust is how you and I become a "we" as we move together through this book.

Introduction

Late in 2018, I was part of a team at Grinnell College that put together a national poll asking Americans a set of questions relating to national identity.[1] Among them was a question about being a "real" American. We asked respondents to rank twelve different traits on a scale from not important to very important.

Topping the list of traits, over 90 percent of respondents reported that believing in treating people equally was essential to being a real American. Approximately 80 percent said that accepting people of different racial and religious backgrounds was also very important.

At the same time, nearly a quarter of people who responded said that having been born in America was very important to being a "real" American. Just as many said that it was very important to be Christian. Approximately 20 percent said that accepting people of different religious and racial backgrounds was not very important to being a real American. I'll call these respondents "nativist."

Based on these numbers, it would be tempting to dismiss nativist American respondents as exceptions to a more general rule of tolerance and acceptance. In a way, that might be the case. But the reality of American life is a lot messier than a poll can capture.

Take, for example, attitudes about American Muslims. About half of the general public has doubts about the extent to which Muslims really want to be part of life in this country and whether they can truly dedicate themselves to American values. These numbers show that it's not just nativist Americans who question whether Muslims can be real Americans.

A good number of people who report believing wholeheartedly in treating all people equally and accepting people from different backgrounds also think that Muslims could be an exception to that rule. I'm not doubting people's sincerity when they report a deep belief in equality and acceptance. But I've been asking myself why so many people see Muslims as a possible exception—and the answer I've come to might not be what you expect.

The attacks of September 11, 2001, traumatized the country. They left us feeling vulnerable and fearful in ways that many Americans had never experienced. Crimes targeting Muslims (and others assumed to be Muslim) skyrocketed once the identities of the attackers became clear. People from across the political and ideological spectrum argued that law enforcement and other security officials should profile Muslims to prevent further attacks. In general, Muslims in the United States entered the national spotlight as never before, often with harmful effects.

It would be easy to draw a straight line from the immediate aftermath of September 11, 2001, to the doubts that many Americans report having about the place of Muslims in the fabric of the country today. In fact, it's *too* easy for us to draw this line. Explaining contemporary anti-Muslim hostility simply as an extension of the fear that many Americans felt after September 11 makes it too easy to avoid asking hard questions about the state of public life in our country.

Anti-Muslim sentiment today is certainly connected to the aftermaths of September 11 and to the fears that reappear every time there is some kind of attack in which someone who is Muslim is involved. But if we take a step back and look at anti-Muslim sentiment as part of a bigger picture, then we can begin to see that the doubts many Americans harbor about whether Muslims can ever be truly American result from something else—something that we must confront together.

The discrepancy between a general commitment to equality and tolerance and specific views regarding where Muslims fit into the fabric of American life comes from fear. Fear is certainly a normal part of being human. It's a rational response to immediate threats, or at least threats we are likely to encounter in our everyday lives. But when our feelings about other people begin to reflect threats that are not part of our everyday experiences, we need to consider where that fear comes from—what's producing it and what makes it stick.[2]

A foundational premise of this book is that widespread fear or suspicion of Muslims results from the corrosive effects of hate—and, more precisely, public hate. Public hate is public speech or activity that draws on and/or perpetuates negative stereotypes about a particular group of people and that encourages others to fear or suspect all members of that group.[3]

In some ways, it might be more appropriate to say that public hate encourages fear of the *idea* of a particular group of people because of what they represent. The stereotypes that are a central part of public hate often have little connection to actual individual people themselves. Yet the effects of fear that results from public hate are very real for the people experiencing them.

When directed toward a particular group—in this case, Muslims—public hate can lead people who think of themselves as tolerant and accepting to adopt attitudes that don't match how they describe their values. And public hate can push people to fear, or at least be suspicious of, people and things in ways that don't match what they're most likely to encounter in their own lives.

Public hate may not lead people to say or do terrible things themselves—though this is certainly a possibility—but it may cause them to be less willing to speak up when they hear or see something that goes against ideals that they otherwise consider very important. This ambivalence is one of the most corrosive effects of public hate.

Public hate can take many forms. It can be longstanding, so baked into history that it's hard for us to see it. It can flare up against a particular group of people because of something that happens. Whatever form it takes, the normalization of public hate is perhaps today's greatest threat to a public life that reflects our stated core values because it makes it difficult, if not impossible, for certain communities to participate in our life together without fear about what might happen to them as they move through their everyday lives. This situation makes equality, as well as real freedom, impossible.

I'm not arguing that as a country we shouldn't pay attention to risks. Everyone deserves to live in safe conditions that make flourishing possible. I *am* arguing that we need to pay very close attention to how closely our fears match risks in our everyday lives. When our fears don't match these risks, it becomes all too easy to move away from our common commitment to equality as a linchpin of our shared public lives.

Building on years of research about anti-Muslim sentiment in the United States, this book offers a case study of public life in our country. It shows what public hate can look like and the ways in which it undermines core American values of equality, tolerance, and freedom. It also shows how, in the face of public hate, American Muslims have created a practical path for public life that many of us can learn from.

In the pages that follow, we will explore the effects of fear on American society, Muslims and non-Muslims alike, and how it has created a need for Muslims to engage the broader American public in specific ways. These efforts at public outreach, in which Muslims seek to humanize themselves, are not entirely voluntary. They are, at least in part, efforts at self-protection in the face of public hate. Despite the hostile environment that has made it necessary for Muslims to put in countless hours of humanizing public engagement and outreach, there are very important lessons non-Muslims can learn from the example they set. We'll talk about how these lessons might translate into small, practical ways that non-Muslims can support Muslims, creating a more welcoming public life for everyone.

Before we get too much further into our examination of anti-Muslim hostility and American Muslim engagement in public life, I want to tell you a little bit about what to expect as we move forward together. We begin in chapter 1 by exploring some concepts and themes that are at the heart of this book. You will also meet Maheen Haq, a young woman from Hagerstown, Maryland, who wrote an article called "Being Muslim

Is . . . ." Maheen serves as something of a touchstone at important moments in the book.

Chapters 2 and 3 identify when public hate against Muslims started to become a more regular feature of public life and explore how public hate has continued to affect the conditions of public life for Muslims in the United States. We will talk about big trends in anti-Muslim sentiment and activity by analyzing significant moments in the emergence of contemporary anti-Muslim activism. We will also meet people who have experienced these trends in their everyday lives.

One of the most challenging decisions in writing this book has been where to put an extended discussion of September 11, 2001. Somewhat counterintuitively, I've decided to locate this material toward the end of the book, in chapter 4. This placement will make it possible for us to consider an explanation of contemporary anti-Muslim hostility that doesn't simply draw a straight line from September 11 to today. Chapter 4 includes reflections on fear, its effects, and how what we do with our fears relates to the kinds of public life we can help to create in our own local communities and beyond.

The discussion of fear and public life leads directly into chapter 5, which looks at the steps that American Muslims communities have taken to push back against anti-Muslim hostility through public outreach and engagement. Just as in chapters 2 and 3, in chapter 5 I draw on media reports to talk about trends in American Muslim public outreach and engagement and to introduce you to amazing people who are trying to resist disturbing developments in our country.

When I first began researching anti-Muslim activity, I didn't anticipate that following Muslim public engagement would become such a significant part of the project. The fact that it's the culminating chapter of the book is very much a reflection of what I've learned in the process.

As my students and I began to collect data about anti-Muslim activity, one of them kept coming across newspaper reports of heartwarming stories about events bringing together Muslim and non-Muslim Americans, often involving interfaith work or other kinds of public outreach by American Muslim communities. Aren't these important to include, too, she asked?

The more I thought about it, the more important it became to me to figure out a way to include these stories. They are just as much a part of our contemporary public life as anti-Muslim activity.[4] Chapter 5 draws on the examples that Muslim public outreach and engagement efforts provide to offer some practical thoughts about what it means to engage in public life in a way that says "hello" to people, that welcomes others into our lives.

I've included additional information about important points raised in the book in a series of notes at the end of the volume. Some of them are brief and just point you to additional sources you could read about a topic if you're interested. Many are much longer—almost like mini essays. These longer notes tell a "scholarly," behind-the-scenes version of what's happening in the main part of the book, focusing especially on key concepts and themes. They are meant to be a resource, but they aren't essential to understanding the core content of the volume. I've already included a couple of such long notes for the preface and for this introduction. There are more in chapter 1, but they decrease in frequency over the course of the book as I introduce fewer concepts and focus more on presenting and analyzing data I've collected.

At the end of the volume, you'll find a list for further reading, which includes short descriptions of the sources I'm recommending as next steps in learning more deeply about the themes we'll discuss in this book.

Now that I've told you about what you'll find as you move through the book, I'd like us to transition to chapter 1 with a little exercise. I invite you to think with me for a moment about something that almost every single person has: your morning routine. Reflecting on something as simple as our morning routine can help us think about some core themes in this book, like citizenship, fear, freedom, and public life.

Wake Up, Fall Out of Bed

When I'm introducing a new topic to students in my classes, I try to con-cretize things by helping them make connections between the material we are discussing and their own lives. For me, this is a really important step toward imagining a life and experiences different from our own—a central goal of this book—because it helps us reflect on things about our own lives that might otherwise remain invisible to us. The following short exercise is similar to one I might do in the classroom.

> *Please think for a moment about your morning routine. We all have one, right? Maybe even put this book down and take a second to jot down what your routine looks like. What do you do before you leave home for school or work or to meet up with a friend?*
>
> *Let's compare notes.*
>
> *I wake up, think about my day, fumble around a little bit as I fall out of bed, wake up my daughter, listen to the news on the radio while I make some breakfast, get dressed, walk my daughter (and the dog) to the bus stop, and then continue on to work.*
>
> *The particulars may be different, but I would guess that the basic elements of most of our morning routines are pretty similar.*

How many of you included in your list having to think about poten-tial harm once you—or your child or your partner—walk out the door? If your response to that question is "me" or "I did," then chances are you don't really need an exercise to help you connect to the material in this book. But for others, pointing out the absence of something can be a powerful way of uncovering things we take for granted.

I never, ever leave my house concerned about what I might run into. I don't have to think about it. I just walk out the door, assuming that ev-erything is going to be just fine. I don't have to consider that the very fact of being out in the world might lead me into an encounter with hostility because of who I am or because of who other people perceive me to be.

In fact, my everyday life is free from these concerns precisely because of who I am, or at least how I imagine people perceive me. My gender and racial appearance and lack of identifiable religious identity make it possible for me to have a morning routine free of concern about what awaits me out in the world.

Yet there are people very, very dear to me—including in my family—who do have to think about encountering hostility when they leave the house. They have helped me, and sometimes pushed me, to reflect on how different it is to live with this possibility rather than to live without it.

It is a very significant difference. The kind of difference that could explain what the young woman you are about to meet calls "fear in your heart."

1

Public Lives

In November 2017, a college student named Maheen Haq published an op-ed in the *Baltimore Sun* called "Being Muslim Is . . . ."[1] I found her writing so moving that when I read it I emailed her immediately and thanked her for sharing her experience. She responded within minutes with a kind message. Months after this exchange her article has stayed with me—maybe more than any other of the thousands of articles I have read while doing research for this book.

In her op-ed, Maheen explains what it feels like to be Muslim in rural Maryland, where she grew up. I encourage you to read the article yourself, but I'll summarize it for you: It's not easy growing up Muslim in rural Maryland. Her everyday experience is littered with indignities. She provides a brief accounting of these experiences by presenting the reader with a list.

To begin, each line starts with "Being Muslim is" and continues with a brief explanation of a particular moment or moments in her everyday life: being flipped off as she drives, having foul diatribes directed at her as she walks down the street, hearing other people at the mall make nasty comments about Muslims that are just loud enough for her to know that they were meant to be heard.

But then the list's style shifts suddenly. The sentences become more abrupt, general statements of what it is like to be Muslim in today's United States. I keep turning over the first of these statements in my mind.

"It is fear in your heart."

For this young woman, being Muslim in her hometown means living with fear in her heart. I have certainly been afraid in specific moments in my life. But this seems so different than living with fear in my heart, the accumulation of painful and scary moments over time. I can only imagine that this kind of fear seeps into almost every part of life.

Maheen goes on to describe how this fear shows itself in her life. Having to apologize for crimes committed by people she doesn't know. Feeling powerless when others call her a terrorist, even though she herself feels terrified by the anti-Muslim hostility that has become such a significant feature of public life in the United States.

She is not without hope. Prompted by a nine-year-old asking how she should respond when someone asks her if she is a terrorist, Maheen wrote her article to express confidence that hard work will bring a better future. She ends the article by pledging to be courageous in the face of fear. She draws on the examples of Eleanor Roosevelt, the Prophet Muhammad, and Martin Luther King to argue that being Muslim requires fighting for justice. She quotes the opening lines of the Declaration of Independence, which establish the fundamental equality of all people, as a call to action in our time.

Reading Maheen's article leaves me feeling hopeful about the future she foresees. Yet doubt enters in when I take a step back and think about it in relation to all of the stories about anti-Muslim hostility I have read over the last few years. Maheen's commitment to what most of us might identify as core American values does not change the reality of our present. The fear that has seeped into her heart is still very real for many people.

That fear has prevented her from being her true self. She has changed the way she looks. She has changed the way she acts so that others see her as nonthreatening and amicable. She has censored herself when it comes to expressing her opinions.

In her article, Maheen labels herself a hypocrite because the answer she gave to the nine-year-old didn't match with her own behavior. When confronted with anti-Muslim hostility, she told the girl, you resist, you break free, you speak your mind. However, Maheen's own confrontation with anti-Muslim hostility had made her forget how to fight, "[h]ow to be unapologetically Muslim, unapologetically confident, empowered and passionate."

I'm confident that Maheen will work with every fiber of her being to be all of these things. Still, it makes me incredibly sad to imagine that her experience of life in her hometown has left her feeling like she needs to be apologetically Muslim, like being her full self will make others question whether she belongs in the only place she has called home.

Of course, Maheen is not alone in this.

Beginning in 2015, Muslims across the country began experiencing greater and greater hostility based on their religious identity—or at least what people assumed to be markers of Muslim religious identity, like headscarves on women, turbans and beards on men, and brown skin. The remarkable diversity of Muslim communities in the United States means that in reality there aren't any characteristics definitively marking someone as Muslim.[2] As a result, in addition to Muslims, many non-Muslims, including Sikh Americans and other people of color, have been targets of anti-Muslim hostility because of gendered and racial or racialized stereotypes about who "seems" Muslim based on a variety of factors, not just physical appearance.

If Maheen's encounters with anti-Muslim sentiment and behavior can serve as an example of what many Muslims in the United States experience with some regularity—and my research certainly suggests that this is the case—then maybe we can begin to imagine the toll this might take on people's lives, both as individuals and as members of a broader American Muslim community. Individual experiences of anti-Muslim hostility affect those individual lives. But the knowledge that anti-Muslim hostility is a more general phenomenon, that Muslims across the country are encountering hateful speech and behavior as well, reinforces and deepens the entire community's expectation of further encounters with hostility.

This is how fear seeps into the heart.

How does this fear affect life for Muslims in the United States? Maheen's story helps us begin to answer to this question. All of the moments she describes as having contributed to the fear in her heart took place in public—they are very much part of the conditions of her public life. Our work begins, then, by looking at this idea: the conditions of our public lives.

The Conditions of Public Life

In perhaps the most famous paragraph in the history of our country, the Declaration of Independence establishes three rights as the building blocks of life in the United States. The words are profound, and their formulation seemingly straightforward: All people have the right to life, liberty, and the pursuit of happiness. Despite the apparent simplicity of this formulation, however, we know that in reality there are lots of different ways that people understand what the words mean.

Something key was missing from my presentation of this famous phrase. In the Declaration itself, a creator God endows all people with these rights. What this means exactly has been at the center of debates for quite some time. It could mean that the people creating a new and experimental form of government intended for religion, or Christianity more specifically, to be at the heart of national public life. Or it could mean that they were underscoring the inalienable nature of these three fundamental rights by referring to a creator God who was nonetheless distant from the everyday life of its creation. The way we interpret this phrase has significant implications for our public lives.

Other parts of the "life, liberty, and the pursuit of happiness" formulation require a fair amount of interpretation as well.

The pursuit of happiness means different things to different people. Some of the philosophers from whom the authors of the Declaration borrowed their ideas would argue that this means we should be free to pursue our own interests with minimal interference. But a "happy" life might also require guaranteed access to some basic building blocks. Identifying just what they are—and who is responsible for providing them—and then balancing this with freedom from interference in our lives is no small task.

Defining happiness, in turn, is fundamentally tied to the way we understand liberty. Prioritizing the ability to pursue our own interests means that we define liberty as negative freedom, or freedom from interference. In contrast, prioritizing access to basic building blocks of a happy life means that we define liberty as positive freedom, because without these essential elements we aren't able to pursue a meaningful life.

How we define life itself, and what it means to protect life, isn't any less challenging. There are very few subjects in the United States today that are more divisive than this. Debates about reproductive choice, so-called stand-your-ground laws, and police shootings all relate in a fundamental way to what happens when one person's right to life appears to conflict with another person's right to pursue their own interests.

The words in the "life, liberty, and the pursuit of happiness" formulation are entirely common. Yet trying to define them is very difficult once you dig just a little bit below the surface—difficult, but crucial. Very rarely do most of us actually engage in debates about defining abstract concepts like liberty or happiness. Instead, we often implicitly define these ideals through the policies and programs we support. Participation in the political system is an important way to demonstrate this support. Voting, though, is only one way that we might express what these abstract ideals mean to us.

We can also attend school board meetings and local planning board hearings; run for office; write letters to the editor or otherwise contribute in some way to public discussions; join a school club, religious institution, or civic organization that addresses pressing needs in our local communities; organize or participate in a protest; or contribute financial resources to national organizations advocating around a particular cause or issue. These are just some examples of the many, many different ways we might go about working toward what we believe to be in the best interests of our communities.

Taken together, all of the different ways that we participate in and support our communities constitute our public lives. By extension, public life consists of all the opportunities we have to work with others to figure out how to move forward as a community on a given issue or set of issues. Public life thus often requires us to work through some pretty hairy disagreements. Given our country's enormous diversity, it shouldn't be all that surprising that disagreements are a big part of public life. Disagreement isn't something we can step back from or wish away. It is our reality, an outgrowth of how our country came to be and how it continues to change, just like everything else around us.

Mediating differences about big ideals and the smaller details in which they play out in our lives is an ongoing process. Our political and civic institutions are all tools we can use to do this work. It is certainly an imperfect process. And so part of our responsibility is to try and make sure that things are working as well as they can in any given moment. All of this mediating and striving—this is the stuff of public life. Mediating our differences is how we end up giving meaning, or definition, to ideals. It's our life together.

Our life together doesn't unfold in the abstract, of course. It unfolds in and through what we can call the conditions of public life.

The conditions of public life are all of the things that affect how much we feel like we belong where we live. Lots of factors contribute to this feeling. To help unpack all the different elements of the conditions of public life, I want to present some concrete examples that might affect whether someone feels like they belong in the public spaces in which our lives play out. I imagine that most of us can connect these examples to our own lives, even if our answers are very different. From there, we can reflect a little on the concept more generally.

Our physical environment certainly plays a role in whether we feel like we belong to the town or city we live in. We notice what the parks look like in our neighborhood and how they compare to others in our town or city. We notice whether the town or city takes care of the streets in our neighborhood. As parents or students, we notice what the schools look like inside and out. The conditions of these elements of our physical environment reflect degrees of belonging to broader communities.

One of the biggest determinants of whether we feel like we belong is interaction with other people. Take, for example, how we experience the ways people respond when we enter public space. Responses can be more or less subtle. Someone could, for example, say nasty or off-color things to you because of who you are (or who they think you are). Or they could say things about you to others just loud enough for you to hear. Sometimes responses can be nonverbal. Police officers and other security personnel might be suspicious about me as I just go about my business and follow me around. Maybe people in my local community have harassed or assaulted you or people you know because of who you are.

At times, other people's behavior that isn't necessary directed at us specifically can still deeply affect whether we feel like we belong in our local communities. For example, when people who live in my local community do things that are meant to make me or people like me feel unwelcome, such as vandalizing a house of worship or a particular business, that affects me personally. When politicians or other public officials say disparaging things about people like me, whether in public or on social media, this affects me personally.

All of these things, from our lived environment and the way that people respond to us when we enter public space to the way that others talk about or treat people like us, constitute the conditions of our public lives. If we don't feel like we belong in our community, we are less likely to actively participate in public life, or at least to participate in ways that are entirely of our own choosing. This has tremendous implications for our everyday lives.

We might be less likely to speak up if our kids aren't getting what they need in school. We might be less likely to attend or speak up at school board meetings or to attend town or city council meetings to voice concerns about something. We might be less likely to report threats or crimes.[3] We might be less likely to run for public office of any kind, whether the school or zoning boards or the town council or county attorney. We might still do some or all of these things, but the reaction from others might range from nothing to nasty looks or comments to harassment or death threats. The experience of American Muslims running for political office, which I will touch on a little later in the book, underscores this last point.

Even when the conditions of public life are challenging for people, this doesn't mean that everything about public life is negative. As we have seen significant rises in anti-Muslim sentiment and activity over the past few years, for example, non-Muslims have also reached out to or publicly say things in support of American Muslim communities.

There are many, many instances of such compassion and empathy. These are good and important moments. But they don't necessarily cancel out the bad. When things are happening to us—or to people we know—that make us feel like we don't belong, our public lives can become uncertain and uncertainty can produce fear. Fear, in turn, will most certainly affect how we live our public lives.

Think back to Maheen, who talks about censoring herself when she disagrees with someone so that she will appear amicable and nonthreatening. Her public self (at the time she wrote her article) is the result of fear, and her fear results from her own experiences and what she assumes others think about her (as a Muslim). These are the conditions of her public life. For Maheen, being what every parent wants for their children—unapologetically confident, empowered, and passionate about who she is and what she thinks—requires an act of courage.

This means that there is a serious problem in the conditions of our public lives. This problem is taking particular shape today, but it has a long history in our country.

Histories and Contemporary Realities of Belonging

Who gets to fully participate in this life together has, from the moment of our country's founding, been a matter of contention. In fact, it's reasonable to argue that the story of our country is very much the story of people claiming the right—and struggling for the right—to be fully a part of public life.

It wasn't simply a matter of language conventions that Thomas Jefferson begins the Declaration of Independence with the idea that all *men* are created equal. "Men" was not a generic term for men and women. It was deliberately restrictive. Nor was "men" a generic term for men of all kinds. In practice—and remember that it is in practice that the reality of ideals come into view—equality applied to white, Protestant, land-owning males. Although the 1790 Naturalization Law granted citizenship to all free white residents, this status certainly did not translate into full participation in public life for everyone who fell into this classification.

Written at a time when there were approximately seven hundred thousand enslaved individuals in what became the United States, the ideals animating the Declaration of Independence most certainly didn't apply to Africans and people of African descent, even if a relatively small number were technically free.

The earliest nonwhite citizens in the United States were those living in territories annexed by the United States at the end of the Mexican-American War in 1848. Over time, other communities of color became eligible for citizenship without stipulations: formerly enslaved peoples with the Fourteenth Amendment in 1868, indigenous peoples in 1924 with the Indian Citizenship Act, and all Asians and people of Asian descent in 1952 with the McCarran-Walter Act.

Even still, citizenship typically did not translate into the ability to fully participate in public life. The history of the United States is littered with examples of groups becoming eligible for citizenship without the right to vote. White women did not become eligible to vote across the country until the passage of the Nineteenth Amendment in 1920 (well before women in other groups who were not yet eligible even for citizenship). It wasn't until the Civil Rights Act of 1964 and the Voting Rights Act of 1965 that individual states were no longer able to restrict voting rights through discriminatory policies that most often affected African Americans.

Citizenship, now almost always linked with voting rights, is an important prerequisite for full participation in public life. The ability to vote in local, state, and national elections is an important formal measure of someone's capacity to take part in the broadest possible range of activities relating to our common lives, to participate in discussions about what really is in the best interest of our communities.

Even recognizing the crucial importance of citizenship and voting, though, we can't assume that these ways of belonging and participating in public life exhaust all possibilities. Plenty of residents of the United States who are not citizens and are not able to vote have very rich public lives, contributing in meaningful ways to their communities. Given that voter turnout for most elections across the country is less than 50 percent, there are clearly also lots of people who could vote who choose to participate in public life in other ways—or not really much at all.[4]

People hope that they can be a part of public life on their own terms and in the ways they want, to honestly and openly advocate for what they believe to be right for their communities and for the country in ways they find most meaningful. This is what Maheen is getting at in her article. She is saying that being able to participate in public life on our own terms, without limits set by other people, is a core element of what it means to be American. She makes it clear that she is committed to this ideal, that being American is an important part of how she thinks about herself and the life she's trying to live.

The vast majority of American Muslims feel very similarly. In 2017, the Pew Foundation conducted a national survey of Muslims living in the United States.[5] Ninety-two percent of respondents indicated that they are proud to be American. More than 60 percent said that they have "a lot" in common with other Americans. Eighty-nine percent reported taking great pride in being Muslim *and* American. A 2016 Institute for Social Policy and Understanding poll shows that 84 percent of American Muslims identify strongly with being American, a number in line with Protestant and Catholic sentiments on the same subject.[6]

These numbers suggest that American Muslims find being American really meaningful. A comprehensive 2017 survey from the same organization found that American Muslims are more satisfied with the country's direction than any other religious group.[7] The gap between Muslims and the general public on this question is quite significant (41 percent to 27 percent). Rates of satisfaction are even higher in individual terms, with nearly 80 percent of those responding to the most recent Pew Foundation study reporting being happy about how things are going in their own lives.

In perhaps the most American of all measures, the vast majority (70 percent) of Muslims in the United States continue to believe that it is possible for most people to get ahead with hard work. This is about 10 percent higher than the public in general.

American Muslim communities are diverse. Survey results certainly differ within and across these communities. African American Muslims, for example, are somewhat less satisfied with the direction of the country and less optimistic about the American dream, a position intimately tied to questions of race in the United States. A *very* small percentage of Muslims living in the United States see some contradiction between their religion and certain American ideals. This tells us that American Muslim communities are a lot like other American communities—that it's incredibly hard to generalize across millions of people on the basis of one shared characteristic, in this case religious identity.

And yet. It's hard to discount the data, which shows that on the whole American Muslims think of themselves—and live their lives—as Americans. We are on solid ground with this generalization.

Given all this evidence, why do so many non-Muslim Americans appear to doubt that American Muslims can be—or want to be—"really" American? And how does this relate to the kind of hostility that has left its mark on Maheen, affecting the way she participates in public life?

The Democracy Fund, a nonpartisan organization in Washington, DC, released a report about stereotypes—positive and negative—that the American public associates with American Muslims.[8] Two points really stuck out to me when I read the report. Only 56 percent of respondents believe that American Muslims want to "fit in" in the United States. And only 51 percent believe that Muslims living in the United

States "respect American ideals." That means that *nearly half the country* thinks that Muslims *aren't* fully committed to being part of life in the United States.

It's hard to discern exactly what survey participants really mean when they respond to questions or prompts. The ambiguity of what it means to "fit in" or "respect American ideals" limits the conclusions we can reach. Still, as much of this book explores, there are very serious consequences that result from nearly half the country thinking that American Muslims aren't fully committed to being American.[9]

Through my own research over the last couple of years, I have found that these sentiments—and the hostility they can lead to—have become part of public life as they never have been before. They show themselves in very local settings and on the national stage, all the way up to the highest elected office in the country.

Back in 2016, then-candidate Donald Trump appeared on Fox News with Sean Hannity not too long after having advocated a freeze on Muslims entering the United States. In response to a question about whether non-Muslims could ever really know, in their hearts, that Muslims immigrating to the United States *really* wanted to be American, Trump said, "Assimilation has been very hard. It's almost—I won't say nonexistent, but it gets pretty close. And I'm talking about second and third generation. They come—they don't—for some reason, there's no real assimilation."

A couple of things jump out in these comments. The default assumption at work is that American Muslims are all immigrants. It's true that American Muslims are more likely than members of other religious groups to have been born outside of the country. A national poll of Muslims living in the United States found that 50 percent are foreign-born.[10] Yet this means that 50 percent of American Muslims were born in the United States, meaning that this is the first and perhaps only home they have ever known. Conflating being Muslim with being an immigrant contributes to a sense of "foreignness" around Islam and Muslims.

His comments further underscore this point when, as something of an afterthought, he extends the argument to those born and raised in the United States. This extension reinforces the idea that Muslims, wherever they are born, aren't and perhaps never can be American simply because they are Muslim. The word "assimilation" is really important here.

Candidate Trump's comments, and the broader attitudes they represent, are not about Muslims believing in the promise of hard work or wanting to be full participants in public life. According to the authors of the Democracy Fund report, the doubts that 50 percent of Americans have about American Muslim commitment to life in the United States reflect concerns about "cultural fit."

Assimilation is a model of becoming—or being—American that emphasizes sameness. It reflects a particular moment in our history of immigration: the arrival of people from Ireland starting in the mid-1800s and from Southern and Eastern Europe a little bit later. These immigrants experienced extraordinary bigotry when they began arriving in large numbers during this period. Over time, however, this changed.

The idea of assimilation often serves as a popular model for thinking about immigration and the process of becoming American. The key element of this story is time. The idea is that eventually, even if they initially encounter bigotry, everyone comes to be accepted as part of the social fabric. However, it's really important to remember that there have always been people in the United States whose ability to be or become truly American has been the subject of debate, often pretty vitriolic and violent. Most often, it's been nonwhites who have been subject to the most extreme forms of doubt and exclusion. As hard as it might be to face, race has always been at the heart of what it means to be American.

From the earliest moments in the country's history, people in positions of power tried to make sure that the boundaries between white and nonwhite were clear. Official efforts include the 1790 naturalization law I mentioned above (to establish the basis for citizenship at the time of the country's founding) and various other laws relating to enslavement, anti-miscegenation, segregation, and immigration. These efforts were all very closely related to questions about who counted as white and who could be American.

It's no coincidence, for example, that in the early twentieth century, just as understandings of what it meant to be white were expanding to include Irish and German immigrants and their descendants, courts were hearing cases about immigrants from South Asia and parts of the Ottoman Empire—including Christians and Muslims—who claimed to be white and, therefore, eligible for naturalization. These cases are especially interesting because what counted as "white" was unclear.[11]

There are a variety of ways judges and other officials determined race. Some looked at skin color. Others drew on biological sciences to make claims about race. Still others thought that "civilizational heritage" determined someone's race. Religion was not allowed to be an explicit element in decisions because of the establishment clause, but it was often a factor in more implicit ways.[12] What was very clear is that being white, or being able to make a reasonable claim to being white, was crucial to the success of those seeking to become American.

The Immigration and Naturalization Act of 1965 changed that, at least officially, by moving away from race as a consideration in setting immigration quotas. If we add this to slightly earlier changes opening citizenship to people of Asian descent, we see that being white was becoming less and less an official requirement for becoming formally American.

In the context of the broader civil rights struggle that was flowering at the national level in the 1960s, these changes show that official policies explicitly linking being American and being white appeared to be coming to an end. As important as these changes have been to what it means to be American—and they have definitely been important—we also need to consider the other ways that communities signal who belongs and who does not. These can be more powerful than official policies.

The "melting pot" story of American immigration suggests that time is the most important factor in the process of becoming American—

being seen as a "cultural fit" for the United States will happen for everyone eventually. Perhaps this view is understandable when we use European immigration as a model. After all, the arrival of immigrants from Southern and Eastern Europe, including Jews, brought on much hand-wringing about whether these "races" could ever become truly American. For the most part, such debates about these particular communities were over by the 1950s and 1960s.

But it's worth considering whether the melting pot is the best model for thinking about American Muslims today, many of whom came to, or were born in, the United States well after immigration reform in 1965 opened the door to immigrants from South Asia, the Middle East, and Africa.

The experience of immigrants from China and Japan, who began arriving in the United States in the nineteenth century, might be closest to what post-1965 Muslim immigrants and their descendants are experiencing today. From the Chinese Exclusion Act of 1862 and the "Yellow Scare" to the internment of Japanese Americans during World War II, immigrants from East Asia and those of East Asian heritage long suffered from the effects of questions about "cultural fit," or the capacity to be truly American.

There are most definitely echoes of these histories in today's debates about the "cultural fit" of American Muslims. This is especially true regarding themes of loyalty and security. We have not seen detentions on the scale of Japanese American internment after Pearl Harbor, but mass detentions of Muslim men after the attacks of September 11, continuing surveillance of American Muslim communities, and efforts to restrict immigration of Muslims all suggest that the reasoning behind past behavior that many Americans view with considerable shame is more alive than we would like to admit.

The more I have studied anti-Muslim hostility, the more I have begun to think that there are other elements of American history that can provide very important insights into what American Muslim communities are experiencing today. Perhaps most important to this story are African

American histories, especially when it comes to questions relating to American Muslims' participation in public life.

African American and Muslim histories are deeply entwined in the United States. Many thousands—it is impossible to know the exact number—of those who arrived as enslaved peoples from West Africa in the eighteenth and nineteenth centuries were Muslim.[13] African American Muslim communities and organizations became targets of FBI surveillance early in the twentieth century because of their open criticism of racism in American society. (The harrowing history of FBI surveillance of African American Muslim communities shows that contemporary relationships between American Muslim communities and law enforcement have deeply fraught roots.) Today, about 20 percent of American Muslims identify as black or African American.[14]

The significance of African American histories to our exploration of anti-Muslim hostility is not limited to African American Muslim history alone, however. African American histories show us that in order to understand the ability of a particular community—or individuals within that community—to most fully participate in public life, we need to look at more than official measures of belonging, like citizenship and the right to vote. Please don't get me wrong: These kinds of measures are *very* important, but they aren't the whole story. Not even close.[15]

Belonging in Public Space

On April 12, 2018, Donte Robinson and Rashon Nelson arrived at a Starbucks for a meeting about a possible real estate investment. Having arrived a couple of minutes early, they decided to wait for the person they were meeting before they ordered. Rashon asked to use the bathroom, which the manager informed him was for paying customers only. A few minutes later, Donte and Rashon were surprised to find three police officers asking them to leave because they were trespassing. When they did not comply because they were still waiting for a potential business partner, the officers arrested them. They waited in detention for nine hours before being released without authorities charging them with anything.

These are the bare-bones facts of the case. There are some other details in dispute. The manager who called the police claims that Donte and Rashon swore at the employee who refused them use of the bathroom. Rashon says that didn't happen. Whatever the case may be when it comes to details like this, it's remarkable that it took only two minutes for Donte and Rashon to arrive at Starbucks, sit down, ask to use the restroom, and have the manager call police to report a case of trespassing.

Two minutes.

In January 2018, the Starbucks Newsroom published a piece called "No Office? No Problem. Meet Me at Starbucks." The article talks about the virtues of using Starbucks as a space to come together, discuss ideas and possibilities, and develop the next big business idea. It quotes company executives talking about the different ways that Starbucks encourages people to use their thousands of locations this way, including offering free wi-fi. The executive is very clear that the company wants Starbucks to serve as a "third place" in communities across the country (and, increasingly, the world)—a space that is neither home nor an office. In other words, public space.

So what happened? Why did Rashon and Donte end up in handcuffs for doing what Starbucks encourages people to do?

The particular Starbucks location in question has a policy that employees should ask people who aren't buying anything to leave the store and to call the police if they refuse. This is not a company-wide policy—in fact, it goes against the general idea of Starbucks as a third space—but locations have discretion to put such guidelines in place. It's possible that the manager who called the police was simply acting on the basis of these guidelines and not because of anything particular about Donte and Rashon.

Starbucks executives seem to think it's not quite that simple. They didn't dismiss the incident as the result of one "bad apple" employee discriminating against certain customers. In the wake of the incident, Starbucks closed all its locations for one day so that employees could attend racial-bias education sessions meant to help prevent discrimination in its stores. Executives took the incident as an opportunity to help employees explore the different ways that discrimination makes its way into our lives, and especially the public lives of people of color. This includes the selective enforcement of policies and rules by businesses and the selective enforcement of laws by municipalities and law enforcement.

The Starbucks incident got a lot of attention in part because someone filmed from the moment police arrived and the video went viral and in part because Starbucks is such a huge part of American life at this point. Similar kinds of things happen all the time in public spaces, though, with significant effects on the ways that African Americans are able to be a part of public life.

Not long ago, I was listening to a podcast called *Stay Tuned with Preet* when a guest unexpectedly brought up the Starbucks incident. The guest, Sherrilyn Ifill, who is the director of the NAACP Legal Defense Fund, said something that has really stuck with me and helped me make an important connection between Rashon and Donte's experience and the subject of anti-Muslim hostility as it relates to public life. It's worth quoting her at length:

> Most of us [African Americans] have had this experience in the public space, of being treated as though we don't belong there, of being treated suspiciously, of being treated as though we were criminals. And it is deeply humiliating. It is an ongoing reminder that we are not regarded as full citizens in many ways, particularly in the public space. And I think many people who aren't black don't understand how the public space is fraught for us because we are always mindful of how we will be treated. And that a central part of the civil rights struggle has been about how African Americans are treated in the public space and the relationship between that and our citizenship.

The connection between citizenship and public space is so important. Ifill makes it clear that wondering how others will treat you when you leave your house and how people will respond to you when you enter public space makes it difficult to be a full participant in public life. It's not just about being in Starbucks. It's about how someone feels in public space and how this relates to their ability to participate in public life when, where, and how it is meaningful to them. This is at the heart of what it means to be a citizen. The connection between feeling a sense of belonging in public space and the ability to freely participate in public life is also at the heart of this book.[16]

Rashon and Donte's arrest is not an isolated incident for African Americans. Public space does not become fraught for entire communities because of an occasional unpleasant experience. Public space becomes fraught over time, when people begin to expect something bad to happen based on their experiences as well as those of their parents, grandparents, siblings, cousins, aunts, uncles, and friends.[17] There is something amiss in public life when public space becomes fraught for entire communities.

* * *

The two examples of Maheen and Rashon and Donte illustrate that there are important parallels between African American and American Muslim experiences of public space. These parallels leave us with serious doubts about using the "melting pot" history of American immigration to think about the present, and future, of American Muslim communities.

The melting pot metaphor suggests that eventually all the different ingredients become largely undifferentiated, with what historian Nell Irvin Painter describes as "symbolic ethnicity" remaining in place to celebrate cultural heritage. This model of becoming American is based largely on the story of European immigrants who became "hyphenated Americans"—Irish-Americans, Italian-Americans, etc. While the melting pot metaphor may work with regard to the experiences of some communities, history indicates that it hasn't applied, and may not ever apply, to communities of color in quite the same way.[18]

If we think back for a moment to Maheen's article, and especially her description of what it feels like to be at the mall, the above passage from Sherrilyn Ifill might very well be about her. I don't mean to suggest that all African American experience is the same as all American Muslim experience. But the sense of feeling unsafe in public space, of being so aware of people looking at you with suspicion, and how these feelings relate to a fundamental sense that many others don't feel like you belong—these are the things that made me immediately think of Maheen when I was listening to the podcast. It made me think of how fear in the heart is something that prevents people from being active in public life on their own terms—that is, from being citizens in the fullest sense of the term.

At the founding moments of our country, political leaders debated whether the full rights of citizenship could ever extend to Muslims. This was a thought exercise (notwithstanding the thousands of enslaved Muslims already present here). They were trying to imagine the outer limits of who could be fully American.[19] They were also debating the same question regarding Africans and people descended from Africans. It is one of our greatest tragedies that these questions persist in our public life. The fact that they persist has a tremendous effect on the extent to which both African Americans and Muslims—or people who others perceive to be Muslim—can be fully citizens of their country.

In the next chapter, we will explore how fear and public hate contribute to conditions of public life in which American Muslims struggle for the right to enjoy full citizenship. We'll focus on the years 2010–2015, a period of time which saw what I call the rehabilitation of public hate toward Muslims in the United States.

2

Rehabilitation of Public Hate

In July 2016, a woman was walking with her two teenage children after having stopped at a Walmart in San Leandro, California. Without warning, two men began pelting her with eggs, apparently commenting on her headscarf during the attack. The two men responsible for the attack will forever remain anonymous. The target of the attack refused to speak with media and declined to move forward with a criminal investigation.

The woman's son immediately snapped a photo with his smartphone and posted about the incident on Instagram, saying,

> My mom is the most kindhearted, loving, and selfless person you'll ever meet. She has a great amount of pride and respect for her religion, culture, and customs. The fact that she can't walk out of her home without feeling safe is sickening. Tonight a couple of guys stalked her out of our local Walmart and attacked her with blows to her head and body with eggs. The reason they thought it was necessary to attack her and my little sister was because they were wearing a hijab. I am at loss for words due to the immense amount of hate that is in this world. No one should have to see their mom broken because of a couple of people having disgusting prejudices about people that do not look like them.

The picture in the Instagram post is haunting. The flash of the smartphone camera illuminates the woman's distraught face in a sea of parking lot darkness. Eggshells sit on top of her head. Yolks and whites ooze down her mauve headscarf and soak her shoulders and chest

The police, who learned of the incident through social media, tracked down the woman a couple of days after it occurred. By their account, she indicated that she was "outraged" by the media attention and had no intention of pursuing the matter further. We'll never know why she didn't want to draw further attention to what happened. The very fact of the news story that appeared about the incident seems like it might violate her wishes. Perhaps my own words right now do the same.

Even with this possibility in mind, however, I'm drawn to write about the incident because it opens onto some really important questions. I hope these questions justify my decision to begin this chapter on anti-Muslim hostility with her story.

The victim is doing something that epitomizes everydayness—she went shopping and was walking to her car, her kids in tow. She is simply going about her own business. She is in public space. Other people decide they have more right to public space than she does. They target her and attack her.

The incident's everyday setting is striking. Something made it possible for such a brazen assault to occur in public space. Something empowered the attackers to feel like it was okay to make others feels unsafe in a space that is supposed to be open to everyone.

It's not possible to know definitively what made the attackers feel justified in what they did without interviewing them. Even then there would be no guarantee that the motivation will be clear. Perhaps more importantly, focusing on the motivation of the individuals involved makes it too easy to avoid looking at the broader conditions that make such attacks possible.

The conditions that made the Walmart parking lot attack possible date back to the years following September 11, 2001. While there were a number of very positive developments relating to Muslims in the United States in the 2000s, including the election of the first American Muslim representatives to Congress, suspicion of Muslims became a significant feature of public life.

And then something changed in late 2015. Suspicion of Muslims became open hostility. Hate crimes skyrocketed to levels unseen since 2001. Elected officials at the local, state, and national levels felt more comfortable making anti-Muslim statements. In 2016, voters elected a candidate for president whose platform included explicitly anti-Muslim policy proposals. Making good on his promises, the newly elected president set about enacting policies targeting Muslims.

Increases in public anti-Muslim hostility in 2015 didn't come out of nowhere. The seeds were set in place in 2010, when anti-Muslim activists began rehabilitating public hate by actively stoking and nurturing fear of Muslims.

Exploring the rehabilitation of anti-Muslim public hate and its effects requires that we cover disturbing material. I want to be very up front about that. As I tried to make clear in the introduction, I recognize that some of you will have more direct experience of anti-Muslim hostility, or similar kinds of discrimination, than others. I hope that my approach to discussing this material will honor these experiences and provide all readers with an opportunity to think about the topic in new ways.

"A Craven Surrender to Political Correctness"

On the morning of March 10, 2011, Representative Peter King, Republican of New York, gaveled a session of the House Committee on Homeland Security to order. The committee had come together for a hearing, which was entitled "The Extent of Radicalization in the American Muslim Community and That Community's Response."[1] King, then chair of the committee, opened the session with some brief comments: "Today's hearing will be the first in a series of hearings dealing with the critical issue of the radicalization of Muslim Americans. I am well aware that the announcement of these hearings has generated considerable controversy and opposition." He continued, "Let me make it clear today that . . . these hearings must go forward—and they will. To back down would be a craven surrender to political correctness and an abdication to what I believe to be the main responsibility of this committee: to protect America from a terrorist attack."

King went on to list a series of individuals living legally in the United States, either as citizens or permanent residents, who had become radicalized. Some of these figures had claimed to be acting in the name of al-Qaʻida. Some had joined or attempted to join al-Shabab, an insurgent group in Somalia.

As King himself pointed out, Obama administration officials had recently expressed concerns about radicalization in American Muslim communities. This was not a concern of Republican lawmakers alone—everyone seemed to agree that this was a topic worthy of investigation. Despite this agreement, there was a fair amount of criticism around how King was framing the hearings and the work of the committee.

Just after King spoke, the ranking Democrat on the committee, Representative Bennie Thompson, weighed in with his thoughts. After brief greetings, Thompson said, "I want to reiterate . . . my belief that a hearing on the linkage between extreme ideology and violent action should be a broad-based examination. Yesterday, the FBI made an arrest in the recent Martin Luther King Day bombing attempt. News reports identified a suspect as a member of the same white supremacist group that influenced Oklahoma City bomber Timothy McVeigh.

"I urge you, Mr. Chairman, to hold a hearing examining the homeland security threat posed by anti-government and white supremacist groups. As the Committee on Homeland Security, our mission is to examine threats to this nation's security. A narrow focus that excludes known threats lacks clarity and may be myopic."

For Thompson, as for other critics of the hearings, the singular focus on radicalization in American Muslim communities was a problem. By not addressing radicalization more generally, Thompson argued, the hearings were overlooking a significant threat to national security—and ran the risk of inflaming anti-Muslim sentiment.

"As members of Congress, our words transcend this room. We must be vigilant that our words and our actions do not inflame," Thompson said. "Acknowledgement of an obligation to be responsible does not equal political correctness."[2]

The references to political correctness point to politicians, including President Obama, who avoid using the term "radical Islamic terrorism" to describe national security threats posed by organizations claiming to act in the name of Islam. For King and others, failure to do so represents an unwillingness to offend Muslims (and liberals) at home and abroad in the face of what they saw as overwhelming evidence that the United States is fighting an existential ideological threat. Critics of the hearings feared that a desire to push back against "political correctness," more than evidence sufficient to justify a narrow investigative focus, had led to a poorly conceived hearing into an important topic. No one in the hearings that day argued that radicalization in American Muslim communities wasn't a subject worthy of investigation. Some committee members and witnesses, though, expressed concern that the hearings—from the title on down—created a distorted picture of American Muslim communities.

To push back against this criticism, Representative King sprinkled in reminders throughout the hearings that he wasn't trying to suggest that all American Muslims were radical. Still, Congressional hearings are often at least as much theater as substance. This is what Congressman Thompson was getting at when he said that the words at the hearing would transcend the room.

Only the very few people who read the entire transcript of the hearing would know of King's statements about what fine citizens most American Muslims really are. The title of the hearings themselves would do most of the work when it came to impressions: "The Extent of Radicalization in the American Muslim Community and That Community's Response."

Writing about these hearings reminds me of the House Committee on Un-American Affairs. This committee hosted hearings throughout the 1940s and 1950s seeking to expose communist infiltration in the US government and American society more generally. The House of Representatives' official historical website refers to the committee's hearings as media spectacles. They often served as an opportunity for members of Congress to portray political opponents as soft on communism more than to discover anything of value. The historical parallels are pretty remarkable, actually.

The King hearings certainly got lots of attention. Close to fifteen hundred items about the hearings appeared in newspapers and magazines across the country that month. They ranged from news articles to feature stories to editorials and op-eds. Many expressed dismay about the hearings and many others offered support for King, praising what they saw as his courageous stand against political correctness.

Looking back at the sheer volume of items about the hearings, I'm not sure that it's all that important whether the majority of those expressing an opinion offered support or expressed opposition. If you hear terms together enough times, in this case "extent of radicalization" and "American Muslim community," the association grows strong. As a statement from an elected Republican official, King's decision to limit the hearings to radicalization in American Muslim communities—and to name them in the way he did—is a far cry from George W. Bush's efforts immediately after September 11 to dampen potential anti-Muslim sentiment.[3]

Something happened in the decade between September 11, 2001, and Representative King's hearings that explains this shift, and set us on the path to the dramatic rise in anti-Muslim sentiment in 2015.

There is clear evidence that in 2015 the United States experienced a rehabilitation of hate in public life. It may seem a little strange to use the word "rehabilitation" here. Usually it has a positive meaning. But I'm using this term quite purposefully because rehabilitation entails an extended period of dedicated work to restore something that has been lost or compromised.

It's worth considering the idea of political correctness in this light.

A Social Movement of Suspicion and Fear

After the worst single terrorist attack in the contiguous United States, it was not widely acceptable to disparage Muslims in public. Even if government policies didn't quite live up to George W. Bush's lofty words, public discourse generally seemed to reflect that idea that it wasn't okay to stereotype entire groups of people. American society had moved on from openly racist public speech. Or so a lot of people thought.

As far as anti-Muslim sentiment is concerned, a collection of activists and organizations worked throughout the 2000s to make it seem perfectly rational—patriotic and virtuous, even—to express suspicion of and hostility toward Muslims in public. The King hearings, coming in early 2011, are among a handful of important examples of how these efforts began to bear fruit, even if they're rather tame compared to what some of the anti-Muslim activists that inspired them were saying and doing.

In *Fear, Inc.*, a 2011 report put out by the Center for American Progress, researchers argue that during the decade between the September 11 attacks and the King hearings a network of anti-Muslim activists and organizations came to exert more and more influence over how Americans perceived Islam and Muslims. *Terrified*, a 2015 book by sociologist Christopher Bail, tells the story of how those active in this network began as fringe voices and over time became mainstream sources of "expertise" about Islam, including for some elected officials and policymakers. I put "expertise" in quotes because very few prominent anti-Muslim activists have particular training in Islamic studies or Muslim history. This makes their ability to influence public discourse around Islam and Muslims all the more remarkable.

Bail argues that the September 11 attacks created a cultural environment in which arguments based on emotion, especially fear and threat, were particularly successful. Using software to look for patterns in thousands of newspaper articles, television transcripts, legislative and policy documents, and social media, Bail makes a compelling argument that anti-Muslim activists and their organizations were successful in using fear to shape public perceptions.

Anti-Muslim activists such as Frank Gaffney, Robert Spencer, David Horowitz, and Pamela Geller argue that violence and a lust for power are at the heart of Islam. (Muslims aren't inherently bad, they argue, but

Islam makes them hate America and Americans.) Each of these activists heads a well-funded organization that distributes a variety of media offering variations on this theme. These include Gaffney's Center for Security Policy, Spencer's Jihad Watch, Horowitz's Freedom Center, and Geller and Spencer's American Freedom Defense Initiative (also known as Stop Islamization of America).

Spend time on their websites, social media feeds, or reading the publications they produce, and you'll find terms like "stealth jihad" and "creeping shari'a." These are key terms and concepts in anti-Muslim discourses in the United States. They suggest that we might not even see the threat coming. This is an especially important approach for fear-based argumentation because it doesn't really require much evidence and yet it's hard, if not impossible, to disprove. One of Bail's most surprising findings offers a case in point. He learned that anti-Muslim discourses seemed to grow in stature during the 2000s the more American Muslim organizations like the Islamic Society of North America (ISNA) or the Council on American Islamic Relations (CAIR) tried to counter them.

The more Muslim activists and organizations try to argue against the claim that Islam is inherently violent and seeks world-wide domination, the more anti-Muslim activists are able to say, "See. They are hiding their true nature." To make their case, anti-Muslim activists point to the Islamic ethical concept of *taqiyya*, or dissimulation. This is the idea that threat of harm based on one's religious beliefs is an acceptable reason to make an exception to the general preference for honesty in all dealings.

Referencing a real Islamic concept, anti-Muslim activists are able to appear like credible sources when they question the sincerity of Muslim denunciations of violence, even if they're distorting the concept beyond recognition. Any attempt by Muslims to correct the record is more evidence of conspiracy.

There is no way to counter this kind of argument.

Anti-Muslim activists often point to a document of dubious origin, allegedly written in 1991 by a member of the Muslim Brotherhood, a sprawling, fractious international organization, as a key piece of evidence of the Muslim conspiracy. This document, the "Explanatory Note of the Overall Strategic Objective of the Organization in North America," claims that the Muslim Brotherhood seeks to undermine Western civilization from within.

This document may very well have been written by someone affiliated with the Muslim Brotherhood. But there is no evidence to support the core claims in the document, including that virtually every major Muslim organization in the United States is a front for a Brotherhood-led effort to take over the country. This hasn't stopped anti-Muslim activists from using the document as a "Rosetta Stone" of stealth Muslim intentions in the United States, which is how Frank Gaffney's Center for Security Policy describes it on its website.

As Bail shows in *Terrified*, the movement of these kinds of arguments into the mainstream happened over the course of a decade. However, it took a particularly combustible development to demonstrate the extent of the anti-Muslim network that had developed over that time. (In this, anti-Muslim activism is a lot like other social movements: slowly building a network and ground game and waiting until just the right situation comes along to assert a very public presence.)

For anti-Muslim activists, a proposed community center in lower Manhattan provided just the right opportunity to resist supposed political correctness and bring anti-Muslim sentiment into the mainstream.

Common Sense and Love for America

In July 2009, a group of investors purchased a long-vacant property about two blocks from the former site of the World Trade Center towers. Among the investors was the Cordoba Initiative, a New York-based non-profit dedicated to interfaith outreach. Soon after, the group announced plans to build a new community center akin to a Jewish Community Center or a YMCA on the site. The facility would also include a Muslim prayer space. Later that year, a local Muslim community began using part of the existing building as a temporary prayer space.

The developers were aware that the location could spark some opposition. They decided to move ahead precisely *because* it was so close to the site of the September 11 attacks. Imam Faisal Abdul Rauf, one of the project leaders, said at the time that a Muslim community center open to and welcoming of all would "send the opposite statement to what happened on 9/11." He continued, "We want to push back against the extremists."

For Pervaz Akhtar, a tailor who lost his shop near the Twin Towers and nearly died on September 11, the project was a test of American freedom. "There is principle involved," he said to a reporter from the *New York Times* in August 2010. "We believe in the American Constitution."

President Obama weighed in on the principles at stake that same month. "As a citizen, and as president, I believe that Muslims have the same right to practice their religion as everyone else in this country. And that includes a right to build a place of worship and a community center on private property in Lower Manhattan, in accord with local laws and ordinances." (He felt compelled to clarify his remarks as statements of principle, not explicit support for the project, when critics began peppering him with comments about pandering to political correctness and questions about his own religious identity.)

City officials, including Mayor Michael Bloomberg and members of the Lower Manhattan Community Board, offered support for the project on the same grounds. The mayor said that property owners ought to be able to do what they want as long as it conforms to building and zoning regulations. Having experienced significant anti-Semitism while growing up in Boston, Bloomberg also pointed to the principles at stake beyond property rights. Referencing first responders at the Twin Towers, he said, "We do not honor their lives by denying the very constitutional rights they died protecting. We honor their lives by defending those rights—and the freedoms the terrorists attacked."

As the project received more and more attention, however, it turned out that lots of people didn't agree. A number of national politicians spoke out against the proposed community center and mosque, including former House speaker Newt Gingrich, Representative John Boehner (House minority leader at the time), and Representative Peter King. Chief among critics of the project was Pamela Geller, conservative blogger and founder of Stop Islamization of America.

Geller had first decried the project in her blog, *Atlas Shrugs*, in December 2009, long before there was much coverage of the project. Much of the post consists of her commentary on a *New York Times* article about it. She suggests that the author of the piece had fallen prey to Muslim misinformation campaigns. In her estimation, the project was nothing but a beachhead for jihadi, political Islam, regardless of what the developers said.

What is perhaps most significant about the post is that it is likely the first time Geller used an argument about the project that would become a staple of opposition in the months that followed: a Muslim community center so close to what had come to be known as Ground Zero would desecrate the site and, in turn, celebrate the tragedy.

At the end of the post, Geller reproduced the final paragraph of the *Times* article. It reads, "Joan Brown Campbell, director of the department of religion at the Chautauqua Institution in upstate New York and former general secretary of the National Council of Churches of Christ USA, who is a supporter of Imam Faisal, acknowledged the possibility of a backlash from those opposed to a Muslim presence at Ground Zero.

"But, she [Campbell] added: 'Building so close is owning the tragedy.'"

Geller closed her post by saying, "That's the point, asshat."

As 2009 turned to 2010, Geller began taking more public steps to speak out against Muslims and Islam. Stop Islamization of America bought ad space on buses across New York City. The ads read, "Fatwa on your head? Is your community or family threatening you? Leaving Islam?" The website listed on the ads urged Muslims to leave the "falsity of Islam." This was the first such ad buy among others across the country. Geller acknowledged that she intended the ads to provoke Muslims.

Even as she branched out into other anti-Muslim activities, Geller was tireless in speaking publicly against the community center in lower

Manhattan throughout 2010. Her blog post on May 6, 2010, "Monster Mosque Pushes Ahead in Shadow of World Trade Center Islamic Death and Destruction," revisited her post from the end of 2009, generating more buzz in the process.

At the root of her argument was the idea that Ground Zero is a grave-yard and living memorial and that a Muslim community center close by—a "monster mosque," as she called it—was fundamentally disre-spectful to the memory of those who died on September 11. It would be, to use another phrase that Geller and other anti-Muslim voices popular-ized, a "victory mosque."

By August 2010, it was clear that a lot of Americans agreed with her, at least to a certain extent.[4] In a *Time* magazine poll conducted August 16 and 17, 27 percent of respondents said that the project was a symbol of religious tolerance, while 44 percent said it was an insult to those who died. (Twenty-seven percent said both were true.) In all, 61 percent of respondents were against the project. Polls just a month later put the number at over 70 percent.

Geller continued to argue that the project was a front for jihadis in-tent on taking over the country. While it's hard to know how many of the 61 percent of Americans opposing the project would have gone that far, general sentiment seemed to suggest that American Muslims did not have the right to "own the tragedy" in the sense intended by Joan Brown Campbell.

In a September 2010 piece appearing in *Human Events*, a popular conservative publication, Geller said that far from being a sign of in-tolerance, opposing the project was simply common sense. "Common sense and love for America."

That same month, Donald Trump spoke out against the community center on *The Late Show with David Letterman*. He said, "I think it's very insensitive to build it there. I think it's not appropriate and insensitive and it shouldn't be built there." When Letterman pressed him, Trump argued that the best solution to the anti-Muslim hatred and vitriol the project was generating was for the developers to move the project. Suspicion of Muslims, he argued, was justifiable because of the association of Muslims and terrorism, and building the project elsewhere would be a great public relations move to create goodwill.

The Park51 project, as the proposed community center came to be known, functioned as a stand-in for larger debates about the place of American Muslims in the United States.[5] Geller was successful in sowing opposition to the community center. Perhaps more significantly, she had pushed forward the troubling idea that suspicion of Muslims and their true motives was a sign of patriotism and love for America. Anything less would be a craven surrender to political correctness.

An amazing 68 percent of respondents to the *Time* poll reported following the Park51 situation somewhat or very closely. This was a national story. Developers eventually abandoned the Park51 project in the face of significant public hostility. While this was certainly a victory for Geller and other project opponents, this was not the most significant outcome.

By leading the charge against the project, which many Americans clearly felt conflicted about (including some Muslims), Geller also pried open space in public discourse for her and her fellow activists' more expansive views about the threat of Muslims and Islam. Stop Islamization of America, the organization she heads with fellow anti-Muslim activist Robert Spencer, began operations in 2010 as a vehicle for disseminating her work.

* * *

This was the backdrop of the King hearings. These are the conditions in which Representative King decided to limit his committee's inquiry to Muslim communities, despite strong evidence that domestic extremism among white nationalists was a significant problem—perhaps more so than radicalization in Muslim communities, according to some committee members. Fear and suspicion, though, don't always reflect the best evidence we have about the threats we face in our everyday lives. Fears and suspicions can often reflect influences other than our own experiences.

The King hearings are just one example of how the efforts of anti-Muslim activists and organizations were succeeding in normalizing suspicion of Muslims and Islam into the mainstream. In the midst of the Park51 controversy, voters in Oklahoma decided that Islam and Muslims posed such a significant and immediate threat that they needed to take action.

People Are Talking . . .

On November 2, 2010, voters in Oklahoma approved State Question 755, a constitutional amendment to ban the consideration of shariʿa in any and all judicial proceedings in the state. The ballot referendum passed overwhelmingly, with 70 percent of the vote. The "Save Our State Amendment," as it was also called, read:

> The Courts . . . when exercising their judicial authority, shall uphold and adhere to the law as provided in the United States Constitution, the Oklahoma Constitution, the United States Code, federal regulations pursuant thereto, established common law, the Oklahoma Statutes and rules promulgated pursuant thereto, and if necessary the law of another state of the United States provided the law of the other state does not include Sharia Law, in making judicial decisions. The courts shall not look to the legal precepts of other nations or cultures. Specifically, the courts shall not consider international or Sharia Law.

In its original form, the ballot as proposed by lawmakers wouldn't have included any definition of shariʿa. The ballot as it actually appeared on November 2 informed voters that "Sharia Law is Islamic law. It is based on two principle sources, the Koran and the teaching of Mohammed."

As someone who has been studying Islamic devotional traditions for over twenty years, I can't imagine sitting down to vote on something like this without more information than that. This is where public discourse becomes so significant. The broader political and cultural environment fills in the gaps. The Park51 controversy was unfolding just as voters in Oklahoma were beginning to consider the Save Our State Amendment.

With 70 percent of Americans voicing disapproval of Park51, we can't reduce opposition to the project to anti-Muslim sentiment. The 27 percent of respondents to the *Time* poll who thought that the project was both a symbol of religious tolerance *and* an insult to those who died on September 11 captures some of the complexity and mixed feelings around the issue.

Still, the suspicion of Muslims that informed the most vocal opposition to the project colored public discourse. This is true whether media outlets were echoing these suspicions or raising questions about claims that Geller and others were making. Suspicion of Muslims and Islam was in the air, and shariʻa had been increasingly functioning as a buzzword for a larger threat to the United States.

Writing back in November 2009 in the *American Thinker*, Geller argued that the failure of political leaders and others to criticize Islam and Muslims and to be honest about the threat they posed was a sign that shariʻa had taken hold of the country. For Geller, this was even worse than mere political correctness. The only possible explanation for the self-censorship she saw around her regarding the Muslim threat was the Islamization of America—shariʻa, which in her estimation forbids any criticism of Islam, had taken hold.

Plain and simple.

Geller was certainly not the only anti-Muslim activist drawing attention to shariʻa, though she was perhaps the most public. Behind the scenes, David Yerushalmi, an activist from Brooklyn, New York, was working hard to convince lawmakers across the country that they needed to act against the creeping threat of shariʻa.

Yerushalmi began his anti-shariʻa activism in 2006, founding the Society of Americans for National Existence. An excellent article in the *New York Times* by Andrea Elliott, "The Man behind the Anti-Shariah Movement," shows that Yerushalmi's work quickly drew the attention of Frank Gaffney, a Reagan-era Defense Department official and head of the Center for Security Policy. This relationship was crucial to Yerushalmi's growing influence, providing significant funding and connections in the political world.

The two men agreed that shari'a posed a significant threat to the United States. Gaffney is best known for arguing that Muslims, like communists in decades past, have infiltrated American institutions with the purpose of undermining them from within. Yerushalmi's quest to ensure that courts don't become complicit in this process proved a good fit.

Together, Gaffney and Yerushalmi recognized the 2009 rise of the Tea Party as an opportunity to bring their anti-shari'a work to the state level. Yerushalmi set out writing "American Laws for American Courts (ALAC)," model legislation banning "foreign law" from judicial proceedings at the state level.

According to Elliott, Gaffney made use of his political connections to talk up ALAC. Among those most interested in the project were the leaders of ACT for America, an anti-Muslim group with local chapters across the country and with strong connections in conservative circles. These efforts quickly began producing results. Local activists across the country recruited representatives at the state level who were willing to introduce versions of ALAC in their legislatures.

In 2010, the year of the Oklahoma amendment referendum, fourteen ALAC-based bills came up for consideration in state legislatures. Three passed. In 2011, the number of bills ballooned to fifty-six. Four passed. From 2012 to 2015, state legislators introduced 110 ALAC-based bills. A total of eleven passed.

It almost doesn't matter that so few bills have successfully passed through legislatures, and that fewer still have been signed into law or passed muster when challenged in court (including the Oklahoma amendment). Back in 2011, Gaffney reported that his and Yerushalmi's goal was to generate discussion about the threat that shari'a poses to the United States and its institutions. They wanted to get people talking. On this front they have been extremely successful.

Their success is especially significant given that there is little to no evidence that there is actually a problem in state courts. Anti-shariʿa activists often point to a 2010 New Jersey case in which a judge denied a woman's request for a restraining order based on her husband's (debatable) claims about his right to spousal sexual access under Islamic law. The decision was quickly overturned on appeal, but like the 1991 document allegedly written by someone associated with the Muslim Brotherhood, one piece of evidence that fits an existing claim can be enough in the context of fear-based argumentation.

Following Oklahoma State Question 755, state lawmakers introducing anti-shariʿa legislation quickly shifted tactics. Drawing on a revised template, legislators filed bills to ban foreign law, rather than shariʿa specifically, from state courts. This helped avoid legal challenges because without any reference to Islamic law it was difficult to prove discriminatory intentions. Despite this change, it was clear that the focus remained the same.

In early 2011, for example, Alaska state representative Carl Gatto introduced House Bill 88. The bill sought to ban the application of foreign law in Alaskan state courts if it would violate rights granted in the US Constitution or protected by state law. Given that courts across the country already follow this practice, why would Gatto, along with legislators in many states, bother introducing such bills? Speaking to the *Anchorage Daily News*, Gatto said, "I'm more concerned about cultures that are vastly different from European immigrants, who come here and prefer to maintain their specific laws from their previous countries, which are in violent conflict with American law."

If there was any doubt about who Gatto was referencing in these somewhat vague comments, the real target of the legislation became all too clear in hearings about the bill in the Alaska House Judiciary Committee. Among the witnesses speaking in favor of the legislation was Pamela Geller. She appeared by phone to discuss the threat of creeping shariʿa in the United States.

Gatto, for his part, freely admitted that he did not introduce the bill because of any real problem in Alaska. He said at the time that he was merely getting out in front of a potential situation. This was and continues to be a pattern across the country when it comes to anti-shari'a legislation. Proponents want to make sure that all newcomers realize that when they come to the United States they need to live according to US law.

When Michigan state representative David Agema introduced a version of ALAC in September 2011, he said, "The people who are angry about this bill obviously have ulterior motives." The greatest of all ulterior motives, he continued, is the imposition of shari'a in American courts. Agema, like many state legislators across the country who introduce ALAC bills, was quick to point out that the bill was a general effort to address foreign law and did not single out Muslims. At the same time, it was clear from his discussion of the bill that Agema was very much focusing on Islam and Muslims.

News coverage of anti-shari'a legislative efforts shows just how similar the approach is in different states. Introduce a bill banning foreign law, then talk about nothing but Islam and Muslims in hearings and media appearances. Repeat if necessary.

When efforts are unsuccessful, especially in states less likely to see anti-shari'a bills become law, legislators claim to have introduced the bill on behalf of a constituent. This tactic is a common response when opponents draw attention to the lack of real evidence that the bills address an existing problem in the state concerned.

These patterns suggest a high degree of coordination. Two examples of bills from 2015 illustrate them.

South Carolina state representative Chip Limehouse introduced an anti-shari'a bill in March 2015. He admitted that he knew of no instances in which someone had tried to introduce an argument based on shari'a in South Carolina courts. Still, he argued, the United States was at war and must take preventive action. Speaking to the *Post and Courier*, a local newspaper, Limehouse said, "You can't predict the future. You never know what might happen." He cited the Center for Security Policy as the chief, and perhaps only, source inspiring his legislative efforts. The bill passed the state House but failed to advance through the Senate.

Just a month later, Maine state representative Michael McClellan introduced a similar bill. Unlike in South Carolina, McClellan's bill did not make it out of committee to the full House. Some committee members complained about a lack of evidence in support of the bill. McClellan claimed that he introduced it on behalf of a constituent.

* * *

Frank Gaffney and David Yerushalmi have been incredibly successful in getting people talking about shari'a. ALAC-inspired bills, whether or not they become law, reinforce what more public actors like Pamela Geller have brought into the mainstream: suspicion of Muslims and Islam.

Gaffney, Yerushalmi, Geller, and other anti-Muslim activists have been much less successful in helping American publics develop a sense of what people mean when they talk about shari'a. Their efforts certainly don't educate non-Muslims about how Muslims in the United States understand shari'a—what they think it is, why it's important to them (or why it's not important to them). They mostly just create fear and a sense of threat.

Anti-shari'a websites typically don't include all that much information about shari'a—how the term relates to legal practice historically, for example, or how and why understandings of shari'a have changed over time in Muslim-majority countries. Instead, these sites tend to reference each other more than anything else, creating a circular system of citations that focus on the threat shari'a plays while leaving the threatening object itself vague and abstract.

Anti-Muslim activists have been remarkably successful in bringing fear and suspicion of Americans into the mainstream since 2010. The gist of what they are saying isn't necessarily that new. People in Western and Southern Europe have been talking about the threat that Muslims pose to Christendom and Western civilization for centuries now. Anti-

Muslim and anti-Islam discourses in the United States echo these longer histories, taking on particular form given contemporary circumstances.

What has changed significantly over the last decade is that these discourses have come to occupy a pretty significant space in public life. More people are talking more loudly about Muslims and Islam in ways that create a toxic environment for American Muslims.

Are You Muslim?

Public discourses, the way that people think about talk about Islam and Muslims in public settings, play out in people's lives in very real ways. One of the benefits of collecting stories about anti-Muslim activity, as I've been doing for a few years, is that I can see connections between national public discourses relating to Muslims and Islam and events that happen to local Muslim communities and to individual Muslims and their families.

Data from August and September 2010 shows a clear connection between what anti-Muslim activists were saying and doing and terrible things that were happening in American Muslims' lives.

As we have seen, by August 2010 opposition to the Park51 project had grown more and more visible. The American Center for Law and Justice, an organization that joined forces with others in the larger anti-Muslim network in the late 2000s, filed suit to block Park51 in early August. Less than two weeks later, President Obama spoke out in apparent favor of the project, citing freedom of religion.

Speaking at the American Enterprise Institute at around the same time, former speaker of the House of Representatives Newt Gingrich argued that many political leaders—like President Obama—were blinded by political correctness, failing to recognize the threat posed by stealth Muslim efforts to undermine the United States. That day, Gingrich called for federal ALAC legislation. He also cited mosques as centers of anti-American activity.

The first anti-Park51 public protest occurred about a week later at the proposed site of the so-called "Ground Zero mosque." It was clear that for many participants the event was about much more than the project itself. Among the most visible signs at the protest were those reading "shari'a" in lettering meant to look like dripping blood.

The same week as the protest, members of the Muslim community in Madera, California, began experiencing the aftershocks of opposition to Park51. People arriving at the Madera Islamic Center found a sign reading "Wake Up America the Enemy Is Here." They soon found another series of signs, including one that read "No Temple for the God of Terrorism at Ground Zero," as well as a brick that someone had thrown at the building. They also found a plastic pig with "Remember 9-11" and "MO HAM MED the PIG" written on its body.

Speaking to the *Los Angeles Times* just after these events, Erica Stuart, a spokeswoman for the local sheriff's department, said, "Obviously, people are connecting this to New York, the debate on whether they should or should not build a mosque near ground zero. But still, here? What in the world does any of this have to do with Madera County?"

The events left members of the Muslim community confused as well. Dr. Mohammad Ashraf, a local doctor, said, "We are not travelers. We live here. We are Americans. We're Rotarians!"

Across the country in August and September 2010, American Muslims were experiencing higher-than-usual rates of anti-Muslim activity. There are media reports of nearly thirty anti-Muslim incidents ranging from discriminatory treatment and property crimes to violent assault during this time. In contrast, there was media coverage of eight incidents during the same months in 2009.

The connection between many of the August and September incidents and the Park51 controversy isn't always as obvious as it was in Madera. But it would be an awful coincidence if anti-Muslim activity increased at precisely the same time that the hateful messages of the loudest opponents of Park51 entered mainstream discourse.

To be clear, just because someone opposed Park51 doesn't mean that they are anti-Muslim. There were very reasonable voices, including some from within Muslim communities and families of those who lost loved ones in the attacks, who thought that the proposed location was too controversial to achieve the planners' original vision of reconciliation and healing. But opposition to the project was taken up by anti-Muslim activists with a much larger agenda. This is what incited others to feel empowered to engage in anti-Muslim activity.

On August, 24, 2010, Michael Enright, a college student, hailed a cab in Manhattan. He began chatting with the driver, Ahmed Sharif. According to reports, Enright said, "Assalamu alaykum," an Arabic greeting meaning "peace be upon you." Enright asked Sharif where he was from, how long he'd been in the states, whether he was Muslim and celebrating Ramadan. When Sharif answered that he was Muslim, Enright said, "Consider this a checkpoint." He then reached through the partition and began stabbing him.

The first wound to Sharif was on his neck, then his arm as he tried to defend himself. Sharif eventually pulled over, got out of his cab, locked Enright inside it, and called the police.

Enright hadn't mentioned Park51, but Sharif himself pointed to a connection. In a statement through the New York Taxi Workers Alliance, he said that the Park51 controversy had made public antagonism toward Muslims very serious and urged his fellow drivers to proceed with great care. "I have been here more than 25 years. I have been driving a taxi more than 15 years. All my four kids were born here. I never feel this hopeless and insecure before," he said in his statement.

Bhairavi Desai, founder and head of the Alliance, reported in an interview with the *Wall Street Journal* that many cab drivers were very nervous. "In light of the Ground Zero mosque debate," he said, "'Are you Muslim?' has taken on new meaning" in talking with customers.

Those who knew Enright were very surprised to hear about what he had done. After all, he was a volunteer with Intersections International, a New York–based interfaith group. So what had led him to attack

Sharif? His lawyers claimed that he was drunk and that he had PTSD from time spent following a childhood friend in the Marines for a college film project. But he had been doing interfaith volunteer work for at least a year. Short of confirmation from Enright himself, we can't really know what set him off, much like we won't ever know with certainty what exactly emboldened the perpetrators of the 2016 anti-Muslim assault in a Walmart parking lot.

It's essential to connect these individual cases to the broader conditions in which they occur. The attack on Ahmed Sharif was not an isolated instance of anti-Muslim activity that month in New York City. Two days later, Omar Rivera, for example, disrupted prayer services in a Long Island City mosque, urinating on rugs and calling those in the room terrorists. It may be tempting to dismiss these events as particular to New York City. After all, this is actually where the Park51 controversy was playing out in real time. But the data on late summer and early fall suggests otherwise.

On August 24, in Carlton, New York, a town of three thousand on the shore of Lake Ontario—about as far culturally, socially, politically, and economically from New York City as any place in the country—five young men shouted slurs from their car outside of a long-established mosque. The driver sideswiped a handful of mosque goers.

Also on August 24, in Mayfield, Kentucky, the zoning board denied the Muslim community's request to build a new mosque.

On August 27, in Murfreesboro, Tennessee, vandals set fire to the proposed site of a new mosque.

On September 3, in Hudson, New York, about 120 miles north of New York City, three men spray-painted anti-Muslim slurs on a mosque in a working-class neighborhood in the small city of seven thousand.

On September 8, in Phoenix, Arizona, vandals spray-painted a mosque that is under construction with anti-Muslim slurs.

On September 10, in East Lansing, Michigan, Muslim community members arrived to find a burned Qur'an on the front steps of their mosque. The pages had been smeared with feces.

On September 11, in Columbus, Ohio, vandals spray painted "9-1-1" on the windows of the Jaffa Market. They also ransacked the store and spray-painted anti-Muslim messages on the counter.

On September 12, in Chicago, Illinois, members of a Muslim community center arrived to find a burned Qur'an on the front steps of their mosque.

On September 21, in Huntington Beach, California, a driver shouted anti-Muslim slurs at a woman named Anwar Hijaz and her sister while stopped at a traffic light. They were both wearing headscarves, which figured centrally in the assaulter's hateful words.

* * *

These are incidents that, for one reason or another, received media attention in late August and early September 2010. Based on the information about them that's publicly available we can't tie these events directly to the Park51 controversy. In some cases, in fact, there are other plausible explanations. The mosque project in Murfreesboro has a long and complicated history. Zoning boards are notoriously hard to please; that's not particular to Mayfield, Kentucky. Perhaps it's also not entirely surprising that anti-Muslim vandalism occurred around the anniversary of September 11.

But let's think for a moment about the broader conditions of public life. Pastor Terry Jones had received a lot amount of media attention when he announced his intention to hold a Qur'an-burning event at his church in Florida to commemorate September 11 and to protest Park51. Well-known political figures argued that the presence of American Muslims posed a "creeping" threat. Anti-Muslim public discourse had become more openly hateful than ever before as anti-Muslim activists linked a building project in lower Manhattan with civilizational conflict.

The spike in anti-Muslim activity in August and September 2010 that accompanied widely disseminated fear-based argumentation around the Park51 project—a controversy that I argue made the contemporary anti-Muslim social movement possible—was a sign of things to come.

Patterns in the data become harder to dismiss when we connect them to individuals who experience them. When the way that people talk about Muslims and Islam in public becomes more hateful, more people feel freer to engage in a whole range of anti-Muslim behavior.

The rehabilitation of public hate has had concrete consequences.

In the four years following 2010, there was media coverage of an average of about seventy instances of anti-Muslim activity per year. This includes what is by now a familiar list of things: harassment, assault, anti-shari'a legislation, politicians trying to score political points by raising suspicion about Muslims in some fashion, legally questionable surveillance of Muslims communities, opposition to mosques and Muslim community centers, vandalism of mosques, and workplace discrimination, among other things.

Each instance of anti-Muslim activity during this time is worthy of our attention. There is always a story to be told. With each anti-Muslim incident, there is someone—or many people—who likely feel less welcome in their own country, less able to participate in public life when, where, why, and how they want. This is the subject of the next chapter.

A Purposeful Omission

Before we move to the next chapter, I want to say a quick word about something I purposefully left out of this chapter that's very related to a larger point I'm trying to make in this book.

I realize that some of you reading may at this point (or perhaps even earlier) be saying, "But Muslims have committed terrorist attacks in the United States. The FBI has busted up other plans before the terrorists have been able to strike. You're overlooking a real threat!" If you are thinking something along those lines, I admit that you're right—kind of.

There are Muslims who have done some really terrible things in the United States, and it's quite possible that sometime in the future there will be other attacks perpetrated by people who claim to be acting in the name of Islam. Terrorist attacks create fear. That's just what they are supposed to do, and it's a perfectly understandable response.

One such attack took place in late 2009, right at the beginning of the period of time we have been talking about. Let me explain why I decided to leave it out of the discussion before this point—and try to make the case for why terrorist attacks don't need to be a big part of our explanation for anti-Muslim hostility.

On November 5, 2009, Nidal Hasan, a psychiatrist in the United States Army Medical Corps, killed thirteen people and injured more than thirty others during a shooting spree at Fort Hood. Although there is no definitive explanation of Hasan's deadly attack, Pamela Geller used it as evidence of the threat of American Muslims in an *American Thinker* article she published shortly after. Absent the widespread notoriety that she gained the next year, though, her words didn't seem to have much immediate effect.

Just as importantly, though, is that the fact of the attack didn't seem to produce a noticeable uptick in anti-Muslim activity, either. Media reports of anti-Muslim incidents from November and December 2009 are more or less consistent with monthly averages over the course of the year (and the years immediately prior).

Ultimately, I decided to leave Hasan's shooting out of the story we have traced in this chapter—at least up until this point. Including it would have reinforced the idea that people engage in anti-Muslim activity only because of, or in response to, something that Muslims have done. By contrast, I am arguing that for the most part people engage in anti-Muslim activity because of the way that anti-Muslim figures talk about Muslims, which in turn profoundly affects public discourse, public policy, and the conditions of public life for Muslims more generally. These are very different explanations and excluding Hasan's attacks from the initial discussion highlights that difference.

Similarly, I decided to not previously include the Boston Marathon bombings on April 15, 2013, carried out by Tamerlan and Dzhokar Tsarnaev. Three people died as a result, with hundreds of others suffering life-altering physical and emotional wounds. The amazing thing? While there were a handful of assaults in which the perpetrators mentioned the bombing, rates of anti-Muslim activity didn't increase much immediately after the attack. The incident didn't become a cause célèbre of anti-Muslim activists, and I think this had a lot to do with why, like the Fort Hood shootings, the bombings didn't lead to an appreciable spike in anti-Muslim activity.

Fear is a very natural response to terrorist attacks. I'm not advocating that we simply turn the other cheek and ignore real threats. What I *am* doing is asking us to think about how our fears relate to or reflect our everyday lives and, when terrible things do happen in communities of which we're part, what we do with our fear over time. That we do have control over. What we decide to do, and whom we decide to listen to, when we are afraid says a lot about what we think being an American citizen means—for us and others.[6] The paths available to us direct our fears. The rehabilitation of public hate made one path more visible to more people by nurturing fear of Muslims.

* * *

This brings us back to the 2016 incident in San Leandro, California, with which I began this chapter. Beyond the facts of the attack, the way that we learned about it also raises troubling questions. The victim happened to be walking with her son. He happened to have his phone either out or readily accessible. He posted to Instagram. Someone reposted to the Muslims of the World Facebook page. A local television station ran a story. But remember, the victim was outraged by the attention. She did not want to pursue any kind of investigation. If it was up to her, no one beyond her family would ever have heard about what happened.

Why would someone remain silent after having this kind of experience? Why would someone decide that it was better for the perpetrators of a nakedly hateful crime to go unpunished than to speak publicly and engage law enforcement? Are there other people in our communities who decide to keep painful incidents to themselves?

These questions relate to the extent to which people feel that public space belongs to them. Access to public space includes feeling that it's possible to walk across a parking lot or down a sidewalk without fear of being attacked based on who you are. But access to public space also includes the extent to which someone feels that they can take up space in public. At a most basic level, taking up space in public means being unafraid to draw attention to oneself by claiming the basic right to be free from fear in public space. At a deeper level, taking up space in public means claiming the right to participate in community debates without fear of backlash.

By the time we come to 2015 in our story of anti-Muslim hostility in the United States, more people felt emboldened to challenge these rights than ever before. The increasing acceptability of anti-Muslim hostility led to an unprecedented policing of Muslims in public space and public life more generally—a development with significant implications for the nature of our lives together.

3

Policing Muslim Public Life

On Wednesday, January 7, 2015, at 11:30 in the morning local time, Chérif and Saïd Kouachi entered the Paris offices of the French satirical magazine *Charlie Hebdo*. They carried automatic weapons, overwhelming security in the building, and proceeded to kill eleven people and injure several others. As they exited the building, they injured a police officer, Ahmed Merabet, in a shootout and then executed him with a single shot to his head as he lay on the ground. The two brothers then fled Paris, eluding immediate capture.

The next day, with the Kouachi brothers still on the loose, Amedy Coulibaly shot and killed police trainee Clarissa Jean-Philippe outside a Jewish school in Montrouge, a southern suburb of Paris. He, too, escaped immediate capture.

With reports that authorities had cornered the Kouachi brothers circulating, word of another incident began to spread. Amedy Coulibaly had resurfaced, taking hostages in a Jewish grocery store in Paris.

Authorities believe that the Kouachi brothers and Coulibaly were in contact as police laid siege to both sites. All three were killed in what appear to have been coordinated raids. Police confirmed that Coulibaly had killed four of his hostages.

Before their deaths, one of the Kouachi brothers told a person whose car they hijacked that they were acting in the name of al-Qaʻida in the Arabian Peninsula, an offshoot of the organization responsible for the September 11 attacks in the United States. Like another Islamist organization that was in ascendency at the time, the Islamic State in Iraq and the Levant (ISIS, or Daesh in Arabic), al-Qaʻida organizations had begun calling on followers to carry out lone-wolf attacks in Western countries.

International sympathy for Parisians, and France more generally, was quick to emerge. Vigils in France and around the world began as early as the evening of January 7. American political leaders voiced sympathy with the people of France. They acknowledged the threat of Islamist movements seeking to harm civilians in Western countries as wars across the Middle East, including Iraq and Syria, raged on.

Meanwhile, anti-Muslim activists in the United States such as Pamela Geller and Robert Spencer got to work using the *Charlie Hebdo* attacks to support their claims that the presence of increasing numbers of Muslims in Europe and North America was part of a "creeping Islamization" of Western societies. This was certainly not a new line of argumentation. The Paris attacks offered another chance to popularize theories of the creeping threat that had up until that point been confined to a very small circle of activists.

This is how 2015 began.

No-Go Zones and the War on Free Speech: Models for Public Life?

As we saw earlier, polling numbers around the Park51 project suggested that people of various political and ideological persuasions were (at least) uncomfortable with a Muslim community center opening so close to the former Twin Towers site. Anti-Muslim activists took advantage of this sentiment to make broader arguments about the incompatibility of Islam and an American way of life, effectively claiming that Muslims couldn't be real Americans unless they gave up Islam.

Familiar anti-Muslim voices began a very similar kind of effort almost immediately after the *Charlie Hebdo* attacks. They focused on two themes. First, they began circulating claims about Muslims willfully refusing to become part of Western societies. Given that about 60 percent of Americans claim to have never met someone who is Muslim, maybe you can see why this claim might have some traction with portions of the American public. Second, and relatedly, anti-Muslim activists used the *Charlie Hebdo* attacks as a wedge to push theories about the incompatibility of Islam and free speech.

On Saturday, January 10, 2015, just one day after the conclusion of the search for the Kouachi brothers and the end of the Paris supermarket siege, Steve Emerson, billed as a terrorism analyst (despite having no such formal training), appeared on *Justice with Judge Jeanine*, a popular opinion show on the Fox News Channel. He claimed that the *Charlie Hebdo* attacks were made possible by the existence of Muslim "no-go zones" in European cities. Law enforcement could not enter these Muslim-dominated areas, in which Muslim vigilantes ran amok implementing shari'a.

In England, Emerson claimed, the entire city of Birmingham had become a Muslim "no-go zone." (This came as quite a surprise to the million-plus residents of the city as well as to the prime minister at the time, David Cameron.) Public pressure quickly forced Emerson to retract his claim, and Fox News offered a correction of sorts as well. Nonetheless, the idea of "no-go zones" had entered into the American lexicon and, the retractions and corrections notwithstanding, anti-Muslim activists and politicians leapt into action.

The governor of Louisiana, Bobby Jindal, for example, discussed no-go zones in a speech in London on Monday, January 19, later claiming to reporters that Muslims were trying to colonize Western countries.

Robert Spencer, who runs a website called Jihad Watch and cofounded Stop Islamization of America/American Freedom Defense Initiative with Pamela Geller, published an article on the FrontPage Magazine website on January 19 doubling down on the no-go zone claim. Versions of this article and interviews with Spencer appeared on other websites in the days and weeks that followed.

For her part, Pamela Geller published an article on the Breitbart website reinforcing the idea that the *Charlie Hebdo* attacks were possible only because no-go zones had made it impossible for French law enforcement to do their jobs.

The idea of no-go zones was not new. Daniel Pipes, founder of Campus Watch, an organization that monitors speech on college and university campuses, began talking about no-go zones in Europe as early as 2006. (After actually visiting areas in question in and around Paris, Pipes retracted his claims.) The term "no-go zones" also came up at a 2007 conference featuring Robert Spencer, and Pamela Geller discussed them in a 2010 interview with the *New York Times*.

As is often the case, Spencer, Geller, and others took grains of truth and wove them together into claims that don't quite hold up under scrutiny.

There have been individuals and very small groups in Muslim communities in France and the United Kingdom who have sought to create enclaves. There are, in fact, informal tribunals that help Muslim families work through disputes about a range of topics relating to family life. Some predominantly Muslim areas in cities, especially in France, have higher rates of crime than others. But none of these things add up to no-go zones.

Muslim communities in France and the United Kingdom, the two countries most frequently appearing in anti-Muslim activist claims about no-go zones, overwhelmingly reject groups clamoring for separation from broader society. Muslim-led tribunals in the United Kingdom that draw on shari'a traditions to provide guidance and adjudicate family disputes are no different from similar bodies available to Jewish and Christian communities.

Law enforcement agencies and local governments around the world struggle with how best to address crime and quality of life issues in areas with high rates of unemployment and where histories of social marginalization continue to affect residents in real ways. Even when faced with evidence to the contrary, though, anti-Muslim activists continued to argue that although "no-go zones" weren't official designations, they existed in practice. (References to no-go zones in Europe and the United States continue to crop up today.) Spencer and Geller portrayed the failure of mainstream media to acknowledge the existence of no-go zones as a willful effort to mislead the American people about the real threat of creeping Islamization.

In their imagination, when it came to no-go zones, the European present was America's future. Their approach to bringing this idea into the mainstream fits a familiar pattern. They took something that most Americans would agree with—that it's important for immigrants and first-generation Americans to become part of American society broadly conceived, even if what this means can vary significantly—and carried it in a very dark direction. This is how anti-Muslim activists are able to cast suspicion so effectively, generating fear that doesn't match the reality of the situation.

The period we're focusing on here, 2015 to 2018, ended just as it began in this regard. On October 30, 2018, Fox News aired a segment repeating long-discredited claims about no-go zones, threats to free speech, and Muslim conspiracies to implement shariʿa in Europe and North America.

* * *

The *Charlie Hebdo* attacks created an opening for anti-Muslim figures to bring the idea of no-go zones into public consciousness. The attacks also generated debates about free speech across Europe and the United States. Some contributions to these debates were genuine, while others were further efforts to cast suspicion on all Muslims.

Charlie Hebdo has a long history of provocative cover art. As a satirical publication, generating discussion through provocation sits at the heart of its mission, and its supporters understand fighting racism to be a central goal of the magazine. Religion and religious authorities are often targets of the magazine's attention.

The publication had courted controversy relating to Islam before. It republished cartoons of the Prophet Muhammad from a 2006 Dutch contest, which itself generated a good degree of controversy. Some of these cartoons depicted Muhammad as a terrorist.

In 2011, the magazine devoted an entire issue to Islam in the wake of Tunisian elections that brought an Islamist party to power. The special issue was called "Charia Hebdo" and had a cartoon of the Prophet on its cover. Just before its publication, unknown attackers firebombed the magazine's offices.

A year later, in 2012, *Charlie Hebdo* again published a series of provocative cartoon depictions of the Prophet Muhammad, this time in the wake of a controversy around the release of a film depicting Muhammad in critical fashion.

All three issues prompted discussions in France around free speech. Some French political leaders as well as representatives of Muslim communities in France were critical. They argued that the decision to repeatedly publish cartoons of the Prophet Muhammad was irresponsible because it deliberately provoked a community that in general felt vulnerable in French society. Others, including a range of French political leaders, identified the magazine as a champion of free speech and a defender of secular French values.

After the 2015 attacks, *Charlie Hebdo*–related debates made their way to the United States as well. One instance, which unfolded at the University of Minnesota, illustrates the complex pressures on communities struggling through questions around public speech that relate to vulnerable groups.

On January 29, a group of University of Minnesota faculty held an event exploring freedom of expression to consider the implications of the attacks. They used a reproduction of the first post-attack *Charlie Hebdo* cover on a poster to advertise the event on campus. The cover featured the words "All is forgiven" and a caricature of a bearded, tearful man wearing a turban and holding a sign reading "Je suis Charlie" ("I am Charlie"), a phrase that came to represent solidarity with the magazine quickly after the attacks. The poster added a red, stamp-like "Censored" over the *Charlie Hebdo* cover image.

The event proceeded as planned. Some months later, though, in May, Inside Higher Ed published an article about a controversy around the event that had remained out of the public eye until then. According to the article, some Muslim students and community members had voiced displeasure about the event's poster to university administrators. They maintained that reproducing the cover was insensitive to Muslims because of closely held beliefs about pictorial depictions of the Prophet. The issue was especially sensitive in this case given the particularly lewd and intentionally provocative nature of images of Muhammad that *Charlie Hebdo* had printed in the past.

Others, including faculty and some senior administrators, argued that reproducing the *Charlie Hebdo* cover was protected speech, illustrating the very point of the event. Removing the image from posters would have constituted a breach of this value, especially given that equity officers did not think that the image violated the university's harassment policy.

What comes through in the article is that the university community genuinely struggled to balance the interests of maintaining protected speech as a core value of intellectual inquiry *and* ensure a safe and inclusive learning environment for all, including vulnerable groups. The conclusion to the affair, which privileged protected speech, may not have pleased everyone involved. But the very fact of what seems to have been a good-faith effort to negotiate a very complex matter reflects a commitment to managing conflict in deliberative fashion.

This stands in stark contrast to an event that occurred just prior to the University of Minnesota debate becoming public.

On May 3, 2015, Pamela Geller was back in the news as she hosted the "Muhammad Art Exhibit and Contest" in Garland, Texas. The event, complete with a $10,000 prize, was meant to antagonize. Given the nature of Geller's previous work, you can perhaps imagine the images the contest attracted and that went up on display. You can Google "Geller Muhammad Art Exhibit and Contest" for a sampling if you are so inclined.

In an email to the *Washington Post* quoted in a May 4 article, Geller acknowledged that she thought about the risk of provocation and suggested that the possibility of violence was well worth it. She said, "I expected that people would come to realize how severely the freedom of speech is threatened today, and how much it needs to be defended. We were prepared for violence."

Toward the end of the event, two gunmen shot an unarmed security guard outside the venue. Local police quickly shot and killed the two men. Just as quickly, Geller identified the attacks as part of a war on free speech.

In a May 9, 2015, article on Breitbart, John Nolte went so far as to say that the exhibition was a "Selma" moment for the "protect free speech movement," referencing the bloodshed accompanying the famous 1965 march for voting rights. He was, in his words, comparing one righteous cause to another.

Geller was also busy in the months leading up to the Muhammad Art Exhibit and Contest, sponsoring another ad campaign in cities across the country featuring posters that read, among other things, "Killing Jews Is Worship That Draws Us Close to Allah."

* * *

The year began with undeniably tragic events in Paris. In the months that followed, we can see very different methods of working through that tragedy—with significant implications for the nature of our public lives together.

One way of addressing the tragedy is evident in the immediate push by anti-Muslim activists to mainstream theories of no-go zones as evidence of the "creeping Muslim threat" almost immediately after the attacks. The attacks served as a pretext to generate suspicion about entire groups of people and to create poisonous conditions of public life for them. The Muhammad Art Exhibit was another effort to use the tragedy to cast further suspicion on Muslims.

The Muhammad Art Exhibit and Contest was the equivalent of a poke in the chest or a finger in the eye of American Muslims. Muslim members of the Garland community voiced concerns about the event based on their closely held beliefs. Other community members worried about public safety. None of these constituencies was a planning partner. The event was clearly meant to provoke the very response it got. It was not in good faith. Quite the opposite.

We will never know exactly why the two men who shot the unarmed guard outside the event space did what they did or what they hoped to accomplish. As noted earlier, there are certainly Muslims who do bad things (as with every other group of people). They appear to have fallen for Geller's trap, making it possible for anti-Muslim activists to draw attention away from the Muslim community members who quietly and respectfully opposed the exhibition.

This was, in effect, an event whose purpose was to show why Muslims aren't *really* American, and thus why non-Muslims need to actively police American Muslim participation in public life to prevent "creeping shari'a." Generating suspicion of Muslims' motives sets the parameters for their participation in public life. Before Muslims have uttered a word about any topic of significance, they are always already tasked with needing to prove themselves as sufficiently American. This is a fundamental distortion of the terms of democratic, participatory public life, and it's one way of understanding the central theme of this chapter: the idea of policing Muslim public life.

The panel on free speech at the University of Minnesota represents a very different way of publicly working through tragedy. The two events may have begun from a similar premise. Both sought to generate public discussion about the nature of free speech and to highlight that freedom of expression is a foundational value in democratic life. The similarities pretty much end there, though.

All reports suggest that the University of Minnesota event was respectful. It certainly wasn't perfect. For example, the Inside Higher Ed article reported that several audience members noted the absence of anyone Muslim on the panel. This is a significant oversight and a real problem, but it's not clear that it reflected an active animosity toward all Muslim voices. The organizers also debated whether to reproduce the

Charlie Hebdo cover, noting that it might have negative effects. They ultimately decided that doing so would be appropriately provocative given the nature of the event.

Accounts of the event make it clear that the intent behind it was to generate honest dialogue. The planning was deliberative in nature, and discussion about the implications of different approaches to publicizing the event continued well after. This shows that the community was committed to thinking about how the event, including its advertising, could affect Muslim students and members of the local public. Such consideration didn't function as a veto of viewpoints holding that other concerns were more pressing. But it does illustrate good faith effort. We should not underestimate the value of acting in good faith, even when the outcome isn't to everyone's liking.

These events in Minnesota and Texas that came in response to the *Charlie Hebdo* attacks illustrate two very different approaches to making difficult decisions about the nature, and possible limits, of public speech. One tried to provide an example of democratic public life—deliberation, consideration of different viewpoints, reflection after the fact about how things might have gone better. The other provoked for provocation's sake, rejecting deliberation and in effect courting violence.

Figuring out what free speech means in practice is actually the stuff of public life—and we need as many voices as possible to be part of this ongoing and often messy work. The University of Minnesota free speech event and the Muhammad Art Exhibit and Contest offer us two very different models of public life that can apply to most any topic of significance.

Certain conditions of public life need to be in place in order for broad and open participation in the work of public life to be possible. Since the beginning of 2015, anti-Muslim sentiment has poisoned the conditions of public life for American Muslims, making such participation very difficult, if not nearly impossible in practice, for the vast majority of people. Anti-Muslim sentiment has created the conditions in which local, state, and federal institutions and fellow citizens police the public lives of American Muslims.

Let's Keep the Big Picture in Mind

For many Americans, the candidacy and presidency of Donald J. Trump were among the biggest, if not the biggest, stories of the period we are discussing. This goes for supporters and critics alike.

Trump's campaign had been full of speeches, policy proposals, and offhand comments that stoked fear and suspicion of Muslims. He questioned whether Muslims could really be American. He implied that Syrian refugees were an army in waiting, a Trojan horse that could strengthen an already creeping Muslim threat. He called for an outright ban on all Muslim immigrants and tourists. He argued that our government should restart "heavy" surveillance of mosques, and he didn't reject the possibility of a registry for all Muslims in the United States, citizens or not.

We can never know to what extent anti-Muslim sentiment motivated people to vote for candidate Trump. At the very least, it's clear that his open anti-Muslim hostility didn't disqualify him from holding the highest elected office in the country. That open hostility toward a group of people didn't disqualify him as a candidate for president reflects the kind of ambivalence that can result from fear and suspicion nurtured by public hate.

I'm not arguing that we shouldn't be talking about the threats that face our country. There *are* members of Muslim communities who seek to harm Americans. In some instances, they are Americans themselves. Candidates for national office need to be able to address the legitimate fears that might result from this threat.

The question is *how* they talk about this threat and to what extent they present the threat relative to other dangers we face in our everyday lives. Some candidates can and do stoke fear and suspicion of all Muslims, contributing to conditions in which people like Maheen Haq live with fear in their hearts. Other candidates try to articulate policies that address extremism in all its forms, as some witnesses and members of Congress urged Representative King to do in his hearings back in 2011.

It's pretty clear which approach candidate Trump took, and President Trump largely stayed the course throughout his first term. For this reason, it's pretty tempting—and quite possible—to make much of our discussion here be about him and his administration.

But that would be a copout.

Yes, President Trump contributed in significant ways to making the conditions of public life for American Muslims quite toxic. News reports of anti-Muslim activity in the months leading up to and following his election show that he made it more acceptable than ever before to target Muslims with hateful, threatening, and intimidating behavior.

On November 15, 2016, for example, a Sudanese American resident of Cedar Rapids, Iowa, returned to his home to find a note taped to the door that read, "You can all go home now. We don't want [n-word] and terrorists here. #Trump."

In the weeks after the election, an identical letter arrived at no less than twelve mosques across the country. After beginning by calling Muslims vile people, the letter goes on to say, "There is a new Sheriff in town—President Donald Trump. He's going to cleanse American and make it shine again. And, he's going to start with you Muslims. He's going to do to you muslims what Hitler did to the jews. You Muslims would be wise to pack your bags and get out of Dodge." It was signed, "Americans for a Better Way."

On December 11, 2016, a man unleashed an anti-Muslim diatribe against a 7-Eleven clerk in New York City. "Don't look at me. I can do whatever I want. You fucking immigrant piece of shit. You Muslim. Go back to your country. That is why Donald Trump is president." He then threatened to have his son stab the man.

On January 30, 2017, just days after President Trump announced his first attempt to restrict the entry of Muslims into the country, Azra Baig, a member of the school board in South Brunswick, New Jersey, overheard another customer in line at Modell's Sporting Goods say loudly in her direction that the Muslim ban was overdue.

Later in the year, on May 3, 2017, Alexander Jennes Downing berated a Muslim family at a public beach on South Padre Island, Texas, taunting them about the superiority of Christianity, the power of Donald Trump, and what it means to be a real American.

On May 6, 2017, a Muslim woman stood in line at a Trader Joe's in Reston, Virginia. Another woman, whom she had actually let in line in front of her, said, "I wish they hadn't let you in the country." The Muslim woman responded that in fact she had been born in the country, to which the second customer responded, "Oh you were?" After a pause, she continued, "Obama's not in office anymore. You don't have a Muslim in there anymore. He's gone. He may be in jail soon, too."

On December 18, 2017, an unknown suspect spray-painted "Trump" (among other things) on a small mosque in Clovis, New Mexico, that serves about twenty families.

These particular incidents offer clear examples of how President Trump's rhetoric and policies contributed to the conditions of public life for American Muslims. The general rise in anti-Muslim activity following the election suggests an effect that goes beyond these explicit examples. As real as this effect has been, though, focusing our attention on him lets *us* off the hook. It makes it too easy to miss the bigger picture—to avoid looking head-on at how pervasive anti-Muslim sentiment has become in our public life.

The role that Donald Trump, as candidate and as president, played in creating the contemporary conditions of public life certainly deserves a fair amount of consideration. But we shouldn't reduce these conditions to him. Candidate and President Trump is not solely or even mostly responsible for the broader policing of Muslim public life.

"They Have a Hard Time Assimilating into Our Country"

The clearest indication that the idea of "no-go zones" had entered mainstream public life following the *Charlie Hebdo* attacks came in mid-February 2015, when two members of the Tennessee state legislature,

Representative Susan Lynn and Senator Bill Ketron, introduced a bill to break up no-go zones in the state.

The bill defined a no-go zone as "a contiguous geographical area consisting of public space or privately-owned public space where community organizing efforts systematically intimidate or exclude the general public or public workers from entering or being present in the area." As the two legislators made clear, there is no mention of Muslims or Muslim communities in the bill.

In comments to the *Tennessean*, which appeared in an article on February 20, Lynn responded to those who claimed that the bill targeted Muslims and that it addressed a nonexistent problem. Of a no-go zone, she said, "You might find it with gang activity, you might find it with organized crime, and of course we have heard that there are some places where it is happening with certain religious groups." Ketron echoed Lynn's sentiments, reporting that they were simply "defining a term that doesn't exist in the law right now."

Neither Lynn nor Ketron claimed to have any experience with no-go zones in Tennessee, though Lynn did pass along that Ketron had told her that he'd "seen it with his own eyes" during a trip to France. But for these lawmakers, as for anti-Muslim activists generally, a lack of direct experience or concrete evidence doesn't mean that something's not a problem. As Lynn told the *Tennessean*, "There are some people who claim that there are some areas of Tennessee where they feel this is happening. And as you know, when there's activity happening where people sort of feel intimidated, there's not exactly a sign up on the wall. But it's just an overall feeling of intimidation."

Similar to Frank Gaffney and David Yerushalmi's goal in promoting anti-shari'a legislation to generate discussion of something that most people didn't think was a problem, it doesn't seem that Lynn or Ketron were primarily concerned about passing good legislation. They wanted people, especially those who had voted for them, to see that they were "protecting" Tennessee from Muslims, even if they couldn't say so out loud.

This tactic was born of experience. Ketron was representing the area around Murfreesboro, a small city southeast of Nashville. It's home to Middle Tennessee State University. It's also home to the Islamic Center of Murfreesboro, which had been at the heart of a controversy a few years before. Just after the Rutherford County Regional Planning Commission approved construction of the mosque in 2010 to provide a permanent worship site for members of the local Muslim community, many of whom had lived in the area for years, televangelist Pat Robertson called it a "mega mosque" and claimed that Muslims were taking over the city.

Opponents quickly filed a lawsuit. They claimed that county officials hadn't given sufficient notice of the planning meeting, violating state law requiring timely announcement of planning meetings in a general circulation newspaper. (The city had in fact published notice of the meeting in the *Murfreesboro Post*, but following established practice had not included an agenda.)

The central argument put forward by the plaintiffs was that Islam is not a real religion, but a political ideology. As a result, they argued, the Tennessee Religious Freedom Act, legislation passed with bipartisan support in 2009 with the express purpose of easing zoning processes for houses or worship, did not apply to Muslims. Had they been able to attend the planning zone meeting they would have objected to the project on these grounds.

The plaintiffs lost their lawsuit and the mosque finally opened in 2012. It had been a bruising process. In addition to the lawsuit, the construction site was vandalized and the city saw an increase in anti-Muslim activity more generally. (To be fair, the Muslim community enjoyed support from others in Murfreesboro throughout the ordeal as well.) The mosque was vandalized again in 2017, an indication that the broader Murfreesboro community continues to work through the consequences of the controversy today.

Beyond the particulars of the case, the lawsuit provides an important window into the evolution of tactics by those seeking to limit American Muslim equal access to public life. Since the lawsuit, claiming that Muslims shouldn't have First Amendment protections under the Constitution has become an increasingly common element of anti-Muslim rhetoric.[1] This argument has not proved a winning legal strategy, though, so legislators and others acting in a public capacity, including citizens at planning zone meetings, often mask the specific intent of their arguments. The broader context of opposition, when in fact it is rooted in anti-Muslim sentiment, often makes this intention fairly clear.

Since 2010, opposition to mosque construction has typically unfolded through the minutiae of planning and zoning, not the expression of some grand ideological vision. Such tactics are on display in many of the fifteen cases of extensive anti-mosque campaigns that received media coverage between 2015 and 2018, a handful of which went on for years.

This was the case, for example, in Bayonne, New Jersey, where the Muslim community had been active in public life for over fifteen years before proposing a mosque and soup kitchen in 2015. They encountered vitriolic anti-Muslim opposition. The federal government initiated an investigation to determine whether the city of Bayonne violated the Religious Land Use and Institutionalized Persons Act in rejecting the project.

Lessons learned from the Murfreesboro lawsuit are evident in Senator Bill Ketron and Representative Susan Lynn's introduction of the "no-go zone" bill. They may not have referenced Muslims specifically, but even a little context makes the intent clear. We can say the same of other anti-Muslim bills that legislators across the country introduced in 2015.

According to the National Conference of State Legislatures, in 2015 twenty states considered legislation that targeted American Muslims in some way. There were multiple attempts in some states. Most of them sought to ban the application of foreign law in state courts. Based on publicly available information, many of these bills followed the American Law for American Courts (ALAC) model, in which there is no specific reference to Islam, Muslims, or shari'a. Outside of the wording of the bills themselves, though, the legislators often made it clear that suspicion of Muslims inspired their efforts.

Speaking to the *Arkansas Times* about his introduction of an ALAC bill in 2015, Arkansas state senator Brandt Smith said,

> When you deal with tribal people or people from other countries that have their own legal system, oftentimes they immigrate to the United States, there are fleeing oppression or they're seeking better opportunities. . . . But in some of these cases, most of these immigrants tend to cluster in areas where there are other people of the same ethnicity and cultural background, so they have a hard time assimilating into our country. . . . In some cases they also bring their problems with them, and they'll bring a legal system with them.

Smith's explanation of the need for anti-shariʿa legislation echoes Lynn and Ketron's "no-go zone" efforts in Tennessee. Smith was careful to avoid specific reference to Muslims. In this particular case, knowing a little bit about legislative activities targeting Muslims in other states goes a long way in developing a sense of what motivated Smith.

Back in Tennessee, state representative Sheila Butt introduced an "anti-indoctrination" bill prohibiting the inclusion of religious doctrines in public school curriculums prior to tenth grade. As with anti-shariʿa legislation, the bill doesn't mention Islam or Muslims explicitly, but, again, a little bit of context, including what supporters said publicly, makes the intent clear.

Parents in districts across the state had begun complaining to school officials about middle school social studies courses that included world religion units, which often incorporate basic information about doctrines and history. Opponents of these curricular elements claimed that students did not have the capacity to distinguish between efforts to teach about non-Christian traditions and indoctrination, making them vulnerable to unwitting influence.

Marsha Blackburn, then a congresswoman from Tennessee before being elected to the Senate in 2018, issued a statement in support of "counter-indoctrination" efforts in public schools. She said, "It is reprehensible that our school system has exhibited this double-standard, more concerned with teaching the practices of Islam than the history of Christianity. Tennessee parents have a right to be outraged and I stand by them in this fight."

A school board in one district proposed a measure empowering parents and other community members to review all curricular materials prior to their distribution to students. This effort came out of parent complaints that a unit in a middle school world history course—which reflected standards put in place by state education officials—was biased in favor of Islam.

With this context in mind, it's hard to imagine that Sheila Butt wasn't targeting Islam with her general "anti-indoctrination" bill. This became even more evident as Tennessee legislators introduced similar bills year after year. An anti-proselytization bill came up for a vote in 2016—and again discussion focused on state social studies education standards around teaching world religions.

Similar attempts to obscure the true intent of anti-Muslim legislation are on display in states across the country in which elected officials introduced ALAC-inspired bills, by far the most common legislative efforts targeting Muslims. In 2015, these legislative efforts included bills in states as culturally and geographically diverse as Maine, Oregon, Mississippi, Colorado, Texas, Delaware, Georgia, Iowa, South Carolina, Minnesota, Kentucky, Pennsylvania, West Virginia, Washington, North Carolina, Montana, and Virginia.

It's very likely that such efforts affected the conditions of public life for American Muslims. They arise out of a fundamental suspicion of Muslims. Even when anti-Muslim bills don't become law—or even make it out of committee—it's important to remember that the goal is to nurture suspicion of Muslims.

Elected officials don't even necessarily need to propose legislation to contribute to toxic conditions for American Muslim participation in public life. Molly White, a Texas state legislator from 2015 to 2017, announced early in 2015 that any Muslim constituent visiting her office would need to renounce terrorism and pledge allegiance to American laws and institutions. White's policy is a blatant example of how anti-Muslim sentiment among elected officials may affect the nature of American Muslim participation in public life.

Instances of anti-Muslim political speech are a clear indication that there are elected representatives—as well as those appointed to serve on behalf of all Americans—across the country who harbor anti-Muslim sentiments, openly questioning whether Muslims can ever *really* become American. Sentiment translates into legislation and other forms of public policy that limit equal access to public life.

Legislative efforts are one significant example of how anti-Muslim sentiment can affect the way that institutions function. They illustrate one significant means of policing Muslim public life. And the same anti-Muslim sentiments driving legislative and other official means of policing Muslims in public life also inspire more immediate, even intimate, forms of anti-Muslim activity that people experience in the course of their everyday lives.

"You're Muslim. You Need to Shut the Fuck Up."

The anti-Muslim activity that people experience in their everyday lives includes a wide range of things. In some instances, people experience anti-Muslim activity that is directed at a local community as a whole. Property crimes targeting Muslims are a prime example.

Think back for a moment to Mohammad Ashraf's reaction to the anti-Muslim activity at his mosque in Madera, California, in 2010. He was perplexed by what he was experiencing. In his own self-understanding, his Americanness was evident in his participation in Rotary, the kind of civic organization long at the heart of public life in local communities. His reaction implies a question: Why would someone target him and his community of Americans? He wasn't personally the target of the vandalism, but it certainly affected his life in profound ways.

There were at least forty media reports of property crimes targeting local Muslim communities across the country in 2015. These include incidents involving mosques as well as Muslim-owned businesses. There were just four media reports of such activity in 2014.

Violent threats directed at mosque communities are another, similar form of anti-Muslim activity. There were media reports of twenty-three such incidents in 2015. These threats arrive in different forms—online posts, emails, voicemails, letters—but they all promise violence, including blowing up mosques and killing Muslims. They rarely target individuals specifically, threatening local communities as a whole and, at times, Muslim communities in the United States more generally.

In one instance in May, just after the Muhammad cartoon contest in Garland, Texas, at least two Muslim communities in Arizona received letters threatening to kill mosque leaders and to burn down mosques across the country. The letters end by saying, "Our people are watching you and patrolling your mosque."

A member of one of the mosques, Imran Siddiqi, told *Arizona Central*, "Normally we brush these off as random incidents." The matter-of-factness of his comment is striking. It indicates that receiving general threats is routine, so much so that Siddiqi appears to expect them as a normal part of his community's life. Yet something here was especially notable for him. The person sending the letter threatened to kill mosque leaders. The addition of these specific threats made him and other members of the community pay closer attention than usual. Based on Siddiqi's comment, this is the only reason we know about this particular threat. But clearly there had been others of a more general nature.

In these examples of property crimes and threats against mosques, the incidents target local communities and, from there, affect individual lives. In other instances, anti-Muslim activity more clearly targets individual Muslims and then become part of a larger story of anti-Muslim activity that in turn affects communities as a whole, whether local or a more "imagined" national Muslim community.

In February 2015, Craig Hicks shot and killed Deah Shaddy Barakat, Yusor Mohammad Abu-Salha, and Razan Mohammad Abu-Salha. They were his next-door neighbors in Chapel Hill, North Carolina. Reports suggested that the killings resulted from a dispute about parking, though Hicks had a history of making anti-religious comments, especially regarding Islam and Muslims. This incident is so outrageous that it marks an extreme end of anti-Muslim activity. Most individuals won't directly experience such violence or even anything approaching it.[2]

The case against Hicks never included hate-crime charges. Prosecutors cited a lack of direct evidence that anti-Muslim hostility led to the killings. The need to have an explicit demonstration of hate highlights a significant problem with using hate crimes as a measure of anti-Muslim activity—it's very difficult to establish motivation or intent. In fact, when determining whether something constitutes a hate crime it may make sense to consider the experience of those targeted. This step is more likely to reflect the effect of a given incident on the lives of people in vulnerable communities.[3]

But there is another problem with using hate crimes as a measure of anti-Muslim activity. Criminal activity targeting individual Muslims, like assault and battery, is less likely to be part of people's everyday experience than other sorts of behavior.[4] It's more likely that people's everyday experiences include the kinds of things that Maheen Haq talked about in her op-ed. Some such incidents receive media attention. The vast, vast majority don't.

A couple of examples from 2015 stick out.

One incident occurred in February in Dearborn, Michigan. A man was speaking Arabic with his kids in a grocery store, only to be accosted by another customer who accused him of being affiliated with ISIS and made other derogatory remarks about Muslims. This isn't criminal. But it doesn't take much imagination to see how this might affect him and his kids negatively by making them feel less secure in their own community.[5]

Still, we will never know for certain how it made the man and his kids feel. Their voices didn't appear in the media report. In some other cases, the voices of those experiencing anti-Muslim activity are at the heart of media reports. These instances provide important insights into how anti-Muslim activity that doesn't rise to the level of criminal behavior affects people.

Another example, which occurred in late May soon after the Muhammad cartoon event, unfolded on an airplane. Airports and airplanes are very common sites for the experience of everyday anti-Muslim activity—so common, in fact, that people use the social media hashtag #flyingwhilemuslim to bring together and highlight all of the different kinds of harassment and ill treatment that Muslims experience while traveling in the United States.[6]

Sometimes #flyingwhilemuslim stories reflect official harassment, such as TSA agents targeting women wearing headscarves for particular attention or men being pulled aside repeatedly by airport security because their name is similar to that of someone on a "no fly" list. At other times, it's simply fellow Americans who police the presence of Muslims in public, shared space.

In May 2015, a passenger on a United Airlines flight named Tahera Ahmad asked for an unopened can of Diet Coke. The flight attendant responded by saying that airline policy wouldn't allow it because an unopened can could be used as a weapon. Tahera pointed out that the flight attendant had just given the man sitting next to her an unopened can of beer. The flight attendant then picked up the beer and opened it. When Tahera looked to fellow passengers to step in and support her, someone said, "You're Muslim. You need to shut the fuck up."

Both of these situations illustrate everyday experiences of anti-Muslim hostility. There are certainly many other possible examples. One particularly gendered experience that comes up with some regularity in media reports are incidents in which people say nasty things about headscarves—in schools, in malls, at stoplights. Again, while this isn't criminal activity, that doesn't make it any less hateful, nor does it make it less likely to profoundly affect someone's sense of belonging or their sense that public space is theirs too.[7]

People's unwillingness to speak up and support her stands out in Tahera's recollection of what unfolded on her flight. The passenger who *did* speak up made her feel unsafe, like her voice and her presence were not welcome in public. These kinds of incidents build over time. They make people wonder if—or when—something more serious will happen.[8] They make it much less likely that people will take up space in public.

We saw earlier how legislative efforts may affect the nature of American Muslim participation in public life. ALAC-style legislation, even when it doesn't become law, signals that articulations of values reflecting shari'a traditions on questions like marriage, divorce, and inheritance aren't welcome in some of the crucial moments in American lives that require interaction with public institutions like courts. This is one way of policing Muslim public life. It sets the terms of engagement with public institutions in a way that limits choices available to most other Americans.

We have also seen a few instances of how anti-Muslim sentiment manifests in the lives of ordinary people. Like anti-Muslim legislation and other forms of public policy, threats against local Muslim communities, violent attacks against individuals, harassment in grocery stores, and nasty encounters on airplanes signal that some non-Muslims actively police the presence, voices, and spoken languages of Muslims in public spaces.

Taken together, these different ways in which anti-Muslim sentiment comes to life create conditions in which American Muslims don't—can't—feel entirely secure in their public lives. This insecurity extends from feeling constrained in interaction with public institutions and worrying about safety in houses of worship to concerns about what might happen if one speaks Arabic in public or fear about speaking up in the face of anti-Muslim sentiment.

It's simply not possible to live fully as a citizen, or even as a resident for that matter, without a baseline access to public space. Public discourses around topics that arouse fear, especially when connected to a particular community, have a significant effect on the public conditions that either enable or restrict access to public space for that group.

"I Think Islam Hates Us"

In November and December 2015, France and the United States experienced two more attacks perpetrated by Muslims. Along with the *Charlie Hebdo* attacks, they served as tragic bookends to frame the year.

On November 13, 2015, attackers killed more than 130 people in coordinated assaults in Paris. The deadliest single incident was at the Bataclan theater, where ninety people were killed. Most of the attackers were French or Belgian nationals. Some had arrived amid the grave refugee and migration crisis resulting from the ongoing wars in Iraq and Syria. Daesh, or ISIS, claimed responsibility.

Less than a month later, on December 2, Syed Rizwan Farook and Tashfeen Malik, a married couple living just outside San Bernardino, California, attacked an event with staffers from the county Department of Health, where Farook was an employee. The two killed fourteen people and seriously injured almost two dozen more. They later died in a shootout with law enforcement. No organization claimed responsibility for the attacks, though evidence emerged that the couple, both of whom were United States citizens, had pledged to carry out such attacks in the preceding months.

From mid-November through the end of 2015, anti-Muslim activity exploded. My students and I found over 140 media reports of anti-Muslim activity in November and December. Many of these reports detail incidents similar to those we've explored—harassment and anti-Muslim speech; assaults; violent threats; vandalism; and incidents on airplanes, including the removal of Muslim passengers.

There had been an increase in anti-Muslim activity following the *Charlie Hebdo* attacks, but the tremendous spike in November and December 2015 was much more striking. Among the notable anti-Muslim activity across the country during these months was a new phenomenon: anti-Muslim refugee fever. Throughout the fall, candidate Trump had been making anti-Muslim comments, some of which were discussed above. Perhaps the most egregious were his comments suggesting that Muslim refugees might be an army in waiting. Given the slippage between native-born, immigrant, and refugee Muslims in the United States in anti-Muslim discourse, Trump's comments were certainly inflammatory. His apparent support in November for the possibility of an all-Muslim database reinforced this slippage.

On December 7, just days after the San Bernardino attacks, the Trump campaign released a statement calling for an indefinite "complete and total shutdown of Muslims entering the United States." This policy proposal was the beginning of a long process that culminated in President Trump's somewhat more limited ban on Muslims entering the country, which finally went into effect in mid-2018 after a lengthy legal battle.

But it would be a mistake to think that candidate Trump was alone in expressing a desire to limit Muslims entering the United States. Governors and local elected officials across the country quickly joined the chorus. In the space of a week in November, more than two dozen governors from states across the country publicly announced that they would refuse the entry of any Syrian refugees to their states. John Cranley, the mayor of Cincinnati, Ohio, declared that his city would not accept any Syrian refugees.

Senator Ted Cruz, running for the Republican nomination for president, announced at a campaign rally that the United States should discriminate against Muslim refugees, opening its arms only to Christians displaced by conflicts in the Middle East.

Representative Steve King of Iowa declared on MSNBC that Keith Ellison, a congressperson from Minnesota and one of two Muslims in

Congress at the time, needed to publicly declare whether he was more committed to the US Constitution or to shari'a.

During a live interview with long-time talk show host Larry King, Representative Loretta Sanchez of California claimed that between 5 and 20 percent of Muslims could be extremists willing to engage in terrorist activity in support of a caliphate and to "go after what they consider Western norms—our way of life."

It was entirely unclear in the interview exactly whom Sanchez was referring to. She may have been talking about people seeking refuge from the conflict in Syria. She may have been referencing Muslim immigrants or native-born American Muslims. She did backtrack and clarify her comments in the days after. But the interview is especially notable because it illustrates the slippage between specific discussions around refugees and security and Muslims more generally.

There is no need to single Sanchez out on this front. The combination of attacks in Paris and San Bernardino at the end of 2015 seems to have made it even more acceptable for elected officials and public figures to make general statements of suspicion about Muslims.

Media reports suggest that 2016 brought unprecedented numbers of such statements. Expressing suspicion of Muslims became more a part of political discourse than ever before—from school board members making explicitly anti-Muslim social media posts to candidates for state and national office questioning whether Muslims could really be American. This was made possible, in part, by anti-refugee fever and the more general association of Muslims with "foreignness."

One telling moment came when candidate Donald Trump sat for an interview with CNN's Anderson Cooper on March 9, 2016. Asked whether the West is at war with Islam—which is admittedly a question that's asking for an imprecise answer—Trump responded, "I think Islam hates us. There is something—there is something there that is a tremendous hatred there. There's a tremendous hatred. We have to get to the bottom of it. There's an unbelievable hatred of us."

Cooper and Trump then had an extended back and forth about terrorism, counterterrorism tactics, fighting Daesh, and controlling who enters the country. The slippage between "Islam," which presumably means all Muslims, and members of an organization, Daesh, that openly embraces tactics meant to terrorize people is startling. It creates quite an association.

Other comments coming from people associated with the Trump campaign further reinforced the sense that all Muslims were suspect. Speaking in June, former speaker of the House of Representatives and Trump representative Newt Gingrich advocated loyalty testing every Muslim in the United States, citizen or not, and deporting those who maintained any devotion to shari'a traditions.

Paul Nehlan, who challenged then-speaker of the House of Representatives Paul Ryan in the 2016 Republican primary, echoed Gingrich. He claimed that Muslims cannot abide by the values of the US Constitution because of their commitment to shari'a and called for a debate about deporting all Muslims.

Republican state legislators across the country continued introducing ALAC-inspired bills and other legislation targeting Muslims, showing that fears of "creeping shari'a" among elected officials remained alive and well.

Democrats weren't immune to the general mood. Former president Bill Clinton, speaking at the Democratic National Convention, included Muslims in his call to people of color to vote Democratic. He said, "If you're a Muslim and you love America and freedom and you hate terror, stay here and help us win and make a future together."

Like the Larry King interview with Representative Loretta Sanchez, it's not clear about whom Clinton was speaking. It's possible that he was referencing Muslim green-card holders in the United States or people on work visas who were seeking to remain in the country. Or perhaps he was talking about refugees. Or perhaps he was talking about American Muslim citizens, who don't actually need to believe anything in particular to remain in their own country, just like every other citizen. While it's unclear who exactly he was referencing, the "us" certainly appeared to not necessarily include American Muslims. The "if" loomed large.

Clinton's invitation to Muslims is not as overtly threatening as some other pronouncements by national political candidates. This doesn't mean, though, that it doesn't contribute to an overall sense that questioning American Muslim commitments to the United States is normal and acceptable. In this way, it is a much more subtle way of policing Muslim public life—it creates an expectation that Muslims need to perform Americanness in particular ways.

Among president-elect Trump's first appointments was Representative Mike Pompeo as the new director of the Central Intelligence Agency. As a member of Congress, Pompeo had been among the most vocal national political voices in claiming that Muslim leaders—in the United States and abroad—have largely been silent in the face of religiously inspired violence and thus share responsibility for such activity. This claim is demonstrably false, but like Clinton's speech it generates a need for American Muslims to prove that "they" don't hate "us."

"This is America. You Shouldn't Be Different from Us."

There's no question that national discourse plays a huge role in contributing to the conditions of public life for American Muslims. Hearing elected officials and candidates running for office in major political parties disparage you or people like you is bound to have a significant effect on your sense of belonging and safety. Yet the things we see and hear at the national level are just as present in local settings.

National discourse and policy proposals may receive more media attention overall. But this doesn't mean that what happens in local communities doesn't also have a profound effect on people's lives. In fact, there is an immediacy to local conditions of public life that we really need to account for as we think about how anti-Muslim sentiment affects the lives—and bodies—of Muslims in the United States.

In May 2016, the small city of Rutland, Vermont, was in the midst of a community-wide debate about whether to move forward with the mayor's proposal to accept up to one hundred refugees from Syria. From the mayor's perspective, as well as that of a sizable portion of the community, welcoming refugees was a way to do some good in the world *and* offset the fact that more and more people are leaving Rutland every year.

Some opponents of the plan expressed concerns about scarce resources and local governance, taking pains to point out that their reluctance to welcome refugees had nothing to do with race or religion. Others, though, mirrored national anti-Muslim political discourses.

On May 12, a group of protesters gathered to voice concerns. Among them was a man named Mark Loseby. Like others, he was frustrated by the mayor's decision to move forward with the plan despite the opposition from some in the community. But his main concern was different.

In an interview with the *Rutland Herald*, he said, "The other part is the refugees—they won't assimilate. What they'll do is they'll get in a community and they'll just group together and they won't blend. They go by Sharia. Sharia law. And they'll actually destabilize the community. Their whole lifestyle is against our Constitution."

Loseby was not speaking from direct experience. There was no Muslim community in Rutland at the time. (Ultimately, only fourteen refugees settled in Rutland before the Trump administration more or less stopped processing refugees.) So where did his views come from? They reflect talk of creeping shari'a, "no-go zones," and a fundamental suspicion of whether Muslims really can be American—staples of anti-Muslim discourses that became more and more a part of public life beginning in 2010.

There is no evidence that such sentiments have led to open harassment of the few families that did arrive in Rutland. But harassment or hate crimes shouldn't be the only measure of how suspicion affects the conditions of public life for Muslims in the small city.

Opposition to refugees ultimately prevented more than a handful from settling in a community that is 96 percent white. This is a recipe for isolation and for these families to remain community curiosities. Maybe this is a harsh assessment. It's important to think, though, about what it takes for people to feel like public space belongs to them—that they have the capacity to decide when, where, and how to participate in public life. What conditions need to be in place for people to feel like being "American" belongs—or could belong—to them?

Having others around who look or sound similarly is one variable that goes a long way in creating a foundation for something like voluntary participation in public life. Being able to speak a familiar language in public or dress in a way that's meaningful without encountering hostility are other factors that can generate a sense of belonging.

Opposition to refugees was a relatively new dimension of anti-Muslim sentiment in the United States, reflecting developments particular to 2015 and 2016. Beyond its effects on the minuscule number of refugees who did gain entry into the country, anti-refugee fever, focusing especially on Muslim refugees, deepened more general suspicion of Muslims in the United States. Speaking Arabic or wearing a headscarf became even more likely to arouse anti-Muslim sentiment or activity.

In September 2016, for example, two women were walking and pushing baby strollers down a street in Brooklyn, New York. Unprovoked, a woman named Emrijeta Xhelili approached them and screamed, "Get the fuck out of America, bitches! This is America. You shouldn't be different from us!" She then grabbed the two women's headscarves and tried to remove them.

This case is almost a caricature of nativist understandings of what it means to be American—except that it's very real. Throughout the year, there were media reports of more than two dozen other violent attacks against Muslims or people the assailants thought were Muslim. Many of the attackers referenced some element of the target's identity, such as their perceived race, and often accused them of being terrorists.

These events represent a fraction of the 127 assaults and 144 instances of ethnic intimidation against Muslims reported in 2016, which we know likely represents a fraction of what was actually happening. All told, law enforcement agencies reported 301 anti-Muslim hate crimes during the year, an increase of 19 percent over the previous year. If we add that increase to the exponential rise in anti-Muslim hate crimes from 2014 to 2015, which came in at 67 percent (from 154 to 267), we start to get a sense of how profound a rise in violent activity we are talking about over a two-year period.

Safety is a baseline condition for someone to feel like public space belongs to them and this, in turn, is an essential component of voluntary participation in public life. Add to this property crimes as well as anti-Muslim activity that doesn't end up in crime statistics, such as employment discrimination, anti-Muslim public speech, anti-mosque campaigns, legislation and other policies at the state and federal levels targeting Muslims, and harassment, and we get a picture of the conditions of public life for American Muslims in 2016.

The number of media reports documenting specific instances of this full range of anti-Muslim activity in 2015 (at least 239) and 2016 (at least 226) are actually quite similar. Month-to-month comparisons across the two years tell a somewhat different, and important, story.

In 2015, nearly 60 percent of these reports came in November (at least eighty-one) and December (at least sixty), coincident with attacks in Paris and San Bernardino and when anti-Muslim suspicion, particularly in regard to refugees, reached fever pitch. Outside of those two months, the average number of media reports documenting anti-Muslim activity per month was about nine and a half. Across 2016, the average number of reports per month was about nineteen. There were only three months in which the number of media reports deviated from this average by more than nine.

Even by these standards, though, November and December 2016 contained hints that the presidential election had further rehabilitated public hate. Instances of anti-Muslim activity increased after the election, with some anti-Muslim activity referencing the president-elect himself as justification. His early appointments included people who had openly expressed anti-Muslim hostility in public. This includes Michael Flynn, who was appointed as national security advisor. Flynn had on numerous occasions said that fearing Muslims was perfectly rational—with the implication that active suspicion of *all* Muslims was entirely understandable and acceptable.

Even before the post-election spike, the data tells us that anti-Muslim activity was likely a much more consistent—routine—part of public life for American Muslims in 2016 than ever before. Even this might not have been enough preparation for what was to come in 2017.

"Do You Have a Green Card?"

In late January 2017, Asma Elhuni was sitting in a cafe in Atlanta. She noticed that a man seemed to be taking her picture. Quite understandably, she asked what he was doing. This is the exchange that followed.

"You like taking pictures of Muslim women? You like taking pictures of me in particular?"

"Are you getting offended?"

"No, I'm just wondering why you have your camera out taking pictures of me."

The man, who identifies himself as Rob, giggles uncomfortably. Then he says, "I asked you a question. Why are you so uptight? What's got you off-kilter?"

"I'd like to know why you're coming in here taking a picture of me."

Rob then proceeds to tell Asma that he thought he saw a famous DJ in the cafe and wanted to take a picture. He said he realized it wasn't who he thought it was, "Then you started acting like a bitch."

"Oh, so now I'm a bitch?"

"You are."

"Because I asked why you're taking a picture of me I'm a bitch."

Rob asked, "Do you have a green card, by the way?"

Taken aback, Asma replied, "Do you think I'm not American?"

Of the nearly four hundred media reports of anti-Muslim activities from 2017, why pick this one? It's not the most outrageous. It wasn't violent. It certainly wasn't the biggest news story of the year. The exchange between Rob and Asma captures something very important about 2017. People with anti-Muslim sentiments felt freer than ever before to make Muslims feel unwelcome in public space.

We can't know whether the story Rob was telling about seeing a DJ was true. Maybe it was. But we can infer a couple of important things from the exchange. First, Asma's experience of being Muslim in the United States was such that it seemed entirely plausible to her that someone would feel free to take pictures of her sitting in a cafe. Second, faced with an uncomfortable interpersonal situation, the dig about Asma's immigration status was so ready at hand that this is where Rob took things. Asma was right. Rob was clearly questioning her Americanness.

It doesn't take a great leap to see why questioning her nationality status seemed to make sense to Rob. Just three days earlier, on January 27, 2017, President Donald Trump took a significant step toward keeping his campaign promise of "a complete and total shutdown of Muslims entering the United States until our country's representatives can figure out what the hell is going on." The new president issued an executive order suspending entrance to the United States for anyone coming from seven Muslim-majority countries, banning Syrian refugees indefinitely, and suspending all refugees from entering the country for 120 days.

A complete Muslim ban it was not. Still, in light of his unconstitutional campaign promise to target a particular religious group for federal action, it took three different versions of the order and over a year and a half of legal battles for the Trump administration to convince federal courts, including the Supreme Court, that national security concerns overrode qualms about the order's potential discrimination.

The first days after the rollout of the executive order were chaotic. There had been no advanced preparation for federal agencies. Customs and border control agents did not have a clear idea of how to implement the new policies. American families with members traveling or living abroad did not know when or if they would be able to see them again. At my small college in Iowa, I had students who didn't know when they would be able to leave the country, to see their families, for fear that they wouldn't be able to come back to school.

The effect of the new policies, whether intentional or not, whether they actually went into effect or not, was that the federal government appeared to be communicating that it really was good and rational to be suspicious and afraid of Muslims. After all, we can't know anyone's immigration or citizenship status just by looking at them, and so anyone who "looks Muslim" became more suspect than ever.

All of the president's talk about lax vetting standards for immigrants and refugees, when seen in the broader context of growing anti-Muslim sentiment in the preceding years, appears to have signaled to a good number of Americans that simply seeing someone who "looked Muslim" was sufficient cause to say something. "If you see something, say something," a ubiquitous call for public vigilance against suspicious behavior, had come to refer to commenting on the presence of certain people in public space.

Rob was not pulling his question out of nowhere. It was a reflection of the increasing acceptance of everyday policing of Muslims in public space.

* * *

In many ways, anti-Muslim activity in 2017 was a continuation, albeit intensified, of much of what you've read about in this chapter.

Legislators across the country continued introducing anti-shari'a bills.

Mosques and Muslim-owned businesses across the country were vandalized, in one case suffering a bombing.

Local Muslim communities continued receiving violent threats by voicemail, email, and letter.

Anti-Muslim activists continued to direct public campaigns at social studies materials and curriculums.

Muslims across the country continued to experience harassment, assaults, and what law enforcement agencies often call "ethnic intimidation."

Political figures at the local, state, and national levels continued to make comments raising suspicions about Muslims in the United States, often about their compatibility with Americanness. In early March, for example, Representative Steven King of Iowa commented on Twitter that Muslim birthrates were undermining Western civilization. "We can't restore our civilization with someone else's babies," he said.

King's comments reflect a familiar, and very gendered, anti-Muslim playbook. In this view, Muslim women pose a threat because they carry babies and foreign culture, both of which transform and thus threaten Western—white—civilization.[9] King's comments are obviously extreme. Yet he made them just weeks after the introduction of the first "Muslim ban" by the Trump administration, which in part sought to prevent Muslim legal residents and citizens from bringing family, including spouses and children, to the United States. Extreme rhetoric and policy don't seem all that far apart on this point.

Aside from cases in which people mention political figures as a motivation for anti-Muslim behavior—and as we saw earlier, there are examples of this phenomenon—it's difficult to do more than establish a correlation between public discourse and everyday instances of anti-Muslim activity. Having said that, though, it's really hard to imagine that repeated attempts to implement what many courts recognized as a "Muslim ban," for example, didn't contribute to poisonous public conditions for Muslims in the United States.

In the month that followed the announcement of a revised version of the Muslim ban, media reports point to what appears to have been a spike in anti-Muslim activity targeting women. In each case, the women were wearing headscarves of some kind, making them a visible target.

These very gendered incidents were not confined to any particular part of the country.

On March 6—the day Trump signed the new version of the ban—a woman approached a Muslim woman in Queens, New York, rattled off some anti-Muslim slurs, and then punched her.

On March 17, a man approached a Muslim woman and her young child in a San Francisco park, made anti-Muslim comments, and then threatened to shoot her.

On March 18, a man approached a Muslim woman in Moorhead, North Dakota, and told her she needed to remove her headscarf before trying to do so himself.

On March 22, a man pulled up beside a Muslim woman breastfeeding her baby in her car in a Charlotte, North Carolina, grocery store parking lot, glared at her from his truck, stepped out of his truck to retrieve a rifle from behind his seat, and pointed the barrel directly at her.

It's possible that the increased frequency of such violent incidents after the introduction of a second version of the Muslim ban was a coincidence. It's also possible that increased awareness of anti-Muslim activity brought more media coverage of such incidents. (The woman in Moorhead indicated in an interview with the *Detroit Lakes Tribune* that this was a more serious variation of a common experience in her life.) Given the preponderance of evidence and the general conditions of public life for American Muslims, though, it seems highly unlikely that this was a coincidence. More people felt more emboldened to act on anti-Muslim sentiment in public—to police the presence of Muslims in public space.

On the whole, anti-Muslim activity in 2017 was more sustained, month to month, than at any other point in the country's history. The average number of reports per month across 2017 was around thirty, up from nineteen the year before. Yet we can't just think about data in monthly or yearly terms. The effects of anti-Muslim activity build over time. They accumulate.

This is why the idea of "policing public life" captures anti-Muslim activity over the four-year period we're considering here. The drumbeat of hostility, from public discourse to everyday experience, is meant to make American Muslims feel unwelcome in public space, to create particular parameters that require Muslims to prove their Americanness above all else. Public participation becomes about ministering to other's fears, making it less possible to engage openly and freely in the *work* of public life. Other people are setting the agenda for Muslim participation—what they can look like, what languages they can speak, and what values they can openly draw on as they live their lives.

Isra Chaker, who leads Oxfam America's refugee campaign, describes the toll this takes. In a November 2018 article in *Teen Vogue*, a go-to source for millennial voices, she says, "Yes, I get tired. We are tired. Too many of us know what it feels like to wake up every morning . . . and be forced to prove that we belong and fight for our rights."

With this requirement at the center of public life for American Muslims, how possible is it to engage freely and openly in policy debates? In these conditions, how critical can average American Muslims be of the country's foreign policy, for example, which has contributed to significant loss of life in Muslim communities around the world? Or of the country's refugee policy, which has led to the lowest number of people resettled in the United States since the United States Refugee Act of 1980 went into effect, a reduction occurring under the cover of anti-Muslim sentiment?

* * *

There were somewhat fewer media reports of anti-Muslim activity in the United States during 2018, though the same kinds of anti-Muslim activities that we saw in the preceding years continued to occur: People vandalized mosques and Muslim-owned businesses; people threatened, harassed, and assaulted Muslims (and people they presumed to be Muslim); public officials made anti-Muslim comments, especially during the 2018 midterm election campaigns; Muslim communities seeking to build or expand houses of worship experienced significant opposition; state legislators introduced ALAC-style bills; a third version of the Muslim ban finally went into effect in June with the blessing of the Supreme Court.

A drop in media reports about anti-Muslim incidents doesn't necessarily mean that the conditions of public life have suddenly improved significantly. In some instances, efforts to exclude Muslims from equal participation in political life have become even more explicit. In two states, Minnesota and Texas, for example, members of local Republican parties actively sought to exclude Muslims. This was especially surprising because both states have growing Muslim communities, suggesting that having at least some Muslims in the party would be important to future electoral success.

During the 2000s, American Muslims, many of whom had been reliable supporters of the GOP up until that point, moved away from the party as anti-Muslim sentiment became a more and more acceptable element of conservative politics. In Minnesota and Texas, local Republican activists appeared to think preventing Muslims from participating in the party was more important than reversing this development.

In January 2018, two Minnesota Republican state legislators and a county-level Republican official posted a message on social media warning of Muslim infiltration in the caucus process, the equivalent of the party primary system in other states. The post came in response to a training session in a mosque; these are common throughout the state leading up to the caucuses, which can be confusing for first-time participants.

According to a January 30 account in the Minnesota *Star Tribune*, the post claimed that an information session at the mosque was about training Muslims to "infiltrate" and "penetrate" American politics to implement a "Muslim political agenda." The post read, "I hope caucus night will be packed by Americans who want to keep American Law and only American Law." Among the elements of the so-called Muslim political agenda that the post mentions? Immigration reform, addressing Islamophobia, and increased money for education.

Later in the year, in Texas, Shahid Shafi became vice-chair of the Tarrant County Republican Party. A surgeon who has served on the city council in Southlake, a suburb of Fort Worth, and as a delegate to the state party convention, Shafi says that he became a Republican because he firmly believes in the importance of keeping government small. Just days after he assumed his post, activists in the county party asked the party chair to remove him because of his Muslim faith. One activist, Dorrie O'Brien, claimed that Shafi advocates imposing shariʻa, supports terrorist organizations, and is simply a "fake Republican" seeking to undermine the party from within. O'Brien also criticized Shafi for not being a sufficiently vocal supporter of Israel.

The call to remove Shafi from his position in the party became a formal motion. Before an early 2019 vote on the motion, party activists behind the effort invited John Guandolo, a former FBI agent and noted anti-Muslim activist, to speak to members about the threat that Muslims pose to the United States.

Prominent Republicans and state party leaders in Minnesota and Texas disavowed the idea that there is any kind of religious test for party membership. But it would be a mistake to dismiss these stories as one-offs. In both cases, "infiltration" and "creeping shariʻa" figure prominently in efforts to prevent Muslim participation in Republic party politics. These are foundational elements of contemporary anti-Muslim activism; these ideas have truly infiltrated the conditions of public life across the country.

These stories about local Republican Party politics represent a new way of policing American Muslim public life. For many Americans, participation in the political process proceeds through parties. Free and voluntary participation in public life requires access to the fullest range of political choices as possible. The same is true of the health of our democracy.

In the 2018 midterm elections, more Muslims ran for public office than had done so since 2000/2001. In fact, Ilhan Omar and Rashida Tlaib, from Minnesota and Michigan, respectively, became the first two Muslim women elected to Congress. But it's important to remember that the elections of Keith Ellison (2007) and André Carson (2008), the first Muslim members of Congress, preceded the worst stretch of anti-Muslim sentiment in the country's history.

That more and more American Muslims are running for office is certainly a positive measure of participation in public life. That the vast, vast majority of American Muslims running for office are doing so as Democrats points to significant divisions in the country that distort participation. I imagine that there are many American Muslims who, like Shahid Shafi, believe in small government and, at least on many policy issues, agree with traditionally conservative positions. A de facto religious test appears to have developed over time, though, affecting participation in the party system.

* * *

From 2010 to 2018, American Muslims experienced more sustained anti-Muslim sentiment and activity than in any other period in American history. It took many different forms, from everyday harassment to national political discourse and policies, all combining, accumulating, to create conditions of public life unsuitable to equal participation in public life for American Muslims.

Fear has loomed large as these conditions have unfolded—fear of Muslims, stoked by anti-Muslim activists who have worked tirelessly to convince the American public that Muslims pose an existential risk to the United States. Life for Muslims in the United States, in turn, has been marked by fear as well—fear of what they may encounter as they go about their everyday lives. The rehabilitation of public hate that began in 2010 has nurtured and made the outsized role of fear in public life possible.

As noted above, there isn't a direct line between the events of September 11, 2001, and the public hate and fear that have been a defining feature of public life since 2010. Still, it's essential to consider how that traumatic moment in the country's history continues to influence our lives together, most especially our fears and their effects.

4

Public Aftermaths of September 11

There is no question that the attacks of September 11, 2001, fundamentally changed the conditions of public life for most everyone living in the United States—and perhaps even the world. It would certainly be easy to point to the attacks and their lasting effects and assume that there's a direct and uncomplicated connection between them and contemporary anti-Muslim hostility. This assumption would be too easy. There is obviously a connection between September 11 and the conditions of our public lives today, but it's neither direct nor uncomplicated.

The September 11 attacks traumatized the country, but they did not destine the rehabilitation of public hate and the outsized role that fear plays in our lives. The attacks did not require that the collective trauma of September 11 play out differently for Muslims and non-Muslims in the United States. As we've seen throughout this book, the contemporary conditions of our public lives—and especially the public lives of American Muslims—are the result of an active campaign to nurture suspicion and fear of Muslims that went public in late 2010.

In the years immediately following September 11, as time passed and the attacks became less present for most Americans, the conditions of public life improved for Muslims in the United States. Hate crimes against Muslims decreased. Nonetheless, the aftereffects of September 11 did create the conditions making the rehabilitation of public hate possible.[1] The United States engaged in multiple wars in Muslim-majority countries, for example, inciting much talk about Muslims being enemies of the nation. These wars, in theory part of a larger War on Terror, helped cement the association of Muslims, Islam, and terrorism for a lot of Americans.

Evidence strongly suggests that the persistence of this association actually makes us all less safe. Since 2010, the threat of right-wing extremist groups in the United States has been increasing. The Department of Homeland Security actually foresaw this trend as early as 2009. According to data from the Global Terrorism Database, white nationalist, anti-government, and other extreme right-wing groups have been involved in more plots than American Muslims since then—and many more such plots came to fruition.[2] Still, the connection between Muslims and terrorism has become a potent and enduring feature of public life in our country.

Researchers at the University of Alabama and Georgia State University have found that that between 2008 and 2016 terroristic incidents perpetrated by Muslims received over 350 percent more media attention in the United States than incidents carried out by other groups or individuals.[3] This both reflects and further contributes to the sense that there is a necessary connection between Muslims and terrorism, but that when others engage in such activity any connection between the perpetrator and a given identity or set of beliefs is incidental.

Where we find ourselves today in this regard was not inevitable. Americans don't naturally see Muslims, both those born in the United States and those who arrived from elsewhere, as a threat to the country. The conditions of public life for American Muslims didn't naturally become so toxic that being Muslim in today's United States is to live with fear in the heart. The attacks of September 11, 2001, didn't in themselves produce this outcome. They did, however, begin clearing the paths that the country has traveled since then.

It's hard to remember life in the United States—and perhaps the world more broadly—before September 11, even for those who were adults at the time. Whether you can recall the events of that day or not, there is no question that the contours of our lives changed that day. The destruction of the Twin Towers, the attack on the Pentagon, the closely averted attack on the Capitol—these developments shattered the myth of fortress America. As a country, we could no longer assume we were safe from attack.

Since then, the idea that we are always under imminent threat of another attack has become a feature of our public life. Fear, a fear that is not necessarily connected to what we are likely to face in our everyday lives, has taken on an outsized role. This has had a profound effect on our collective life. The idea of constant threat makes us more willing to accept changes in our public lives. Some of these changes, like longer security lines at the airport, aren't more than minor annoyances (unless you are regularly subject to random screenings).

But other changes, such as the government having more and more access to more and more data about us, have changed our lives profoundly. There are legitimate questions about whether this is good for us in the long run.

In the months after the attacks, our representatives in Washington remade the national security apparatus, creating the Department of Homeland Security. Law enforcement agencies across the country increased their intelligence gathering capabilities and became much more militarized in their appearance and approach to policing. While we continue to debate tradeoffs between security and civil liberties, the specter of terrorism has changed this formula considerably. We were a national community traumatized by events that had been unthinkable before that moment.

Often, we think of trauma as something that individuals experience. We have a painful experience and we continue to feel the emotional and psychological effects for a long time. But what happens when something so big happens that it affects lots of people at the same time? Trauma is something that people share—trauma can be social rather than individual.

Sociologists call this "community" or "cultural trauma." It results from a shock to the collective system from an event or events that profoundly change(s) what a community has come to expect out of life, or what feels like normal or routine. The attacks of September 2001 provided this kind of shock.[4] A new routine of public life, a new normal, began to emerge out of this trauma. This new normal is a routine that changed the conditions of public life in considerable—and in some important respects different—ways for people across the country.

Suspicion as a New Normal

The weeks and months following the attacks were chaotic. No one knew how a small group of men had entered the United States, gone unsuspected while planning massive attacks, and successfully carried out such horrendous crimes. Norms of public life were suspended in the search for answers, beginning with the work of the federal government. As Mindy Tucker, a spokesperson at the Department of Justice, said to the *New York Times*, "September 11 has forced the entire federal government to change the way we do business."

In our own lives, it's a pretty good rule of thumb to avoid making big changes in times of crisis. But the enormity of the attacks in human terms and what they represented to national self-understanding made it impossible to follow this advice when it came to the federal government's response. The effects of these changes continue to unfold today.

Within weeks, Congress had passed the USA Patriot Act, which transformed the government's power of surveillance, broadened the bases upon which law enforcement and intelligence agencies could pursue investigations, and increased the number of crimes situated under the broad umbrella of material support for terrorism.

Just after the attacks, the FBI engaged in a dragnet operation to identify potential threats to national security. The available numbers vary, but the FBI detained as many as twelve hundred men during this period based on their race, religion, immigration status, and/or national origin. None of the detainees turned out to have any connection to or knowledge of the attacks. No terrorism-related charges resulted from the detentions.

Some of those detained were charged with civil immigration infractions and released with the understanding that they would voluntarily leave the country. Others were charged with minor, nonviolent offenses and released. Most ended up spending months in detention without any charges.

Many of those detained were housed in a facility in Brooklyn, New York. Treatment at the Administrative Maximum Special Housing Unit of the Metropolitan Detention Center was so harsh that a number of detainees filed a class action lawsuit against those responsible for the dragnet operation, including the attorney general at the time, John Ashcroft.

The Supreme Court ultimately ruled against the plaintiffs. But the lawsuit shed light on the terrible treatment of detainees, including physical and psychological abuse.

The period just after the attacks also saw the creation of a new entity, the Office of Homeland Security, which was meant to help coordinate anti-terrorism operations across the federal government. A little over a year later, in 2002, Congress passed the Homeland Security Act, creating the Department of Homeland Security (DHS). The act consolidated twenty-two different offices and agencies into one department, introducing some significant changes along the way. US Immigration and Customs Enforcement (ICE) and a revamped Transportation and Security Administration (TSA) emerged from this reorganization.

Counterterrorism is at the heart of Homeland Security's responsibilities. The department is supposed to prevent terrorist attacks, an agenda that has required a massive expansion of intelligence gathering and the introduction of a new emphasis in federal law enforcement efforts. Federal law enforcement officials are no longer just responsible for investigating, apprehending, and charging people who have already (allegedly) committed criminal acts. Identifying and tracking people who *might* engage in criminal activity relating to national security has become a much more significant focus.

Surveillance of potential threats to public order has always been part of the federal government's work, especially the FBI's. The FBI has followed, listened in on, and harassed communists, socialists, union leaders, and civil rights activists, to name just a few targets over the years. The FBI began surveilling Muslim communities in the United States, such as African American groups like the Moorish Science Temple and the Nation of Islam, as early as the 1920s and 1930s.

Today, Muslim communities across the country simply assume that they are under surveillance by the FBI.[5] It's important to note, though, that the post–September 11 expansion of intelligence gathering and surveillance targeting Muslims in the United States was not limited to the federal government.

In New York City, the NYPD expanded its intelligence gathering and analysis, signaling an extension of its mission into prevention similar to changes at the federal level. Officials revamped an existing intelligence bureau and created an in-house counterterrorism operation. As has now become public record, the NYPD embarked on unprecedented surveillance of Muslim communities. It monitored mosques, schools, cafes, corner stores—anywhere that Muslims congregated as they went about their everyday lives.

At the center of this effort was the Demographics Unit. Officers in the unit mapped the city, identifying areas with concentrations of Muslim residents which then became the focus of heavy surveillance. Using electronic monitoring and undercover officers, the unit created files on Muslims throughout the city, detailing their everyday lives. This work was not based on any evidence of wrongdoing and produced no actionable intelligence. The NYPD has since disbanded the unit.

Nor were such efforts limited to New York City. In early 2018, the NYPD settled a lawsuit that alleged its surveillance activities extended to surrounding states. Plaintiffs in the suit claimed that the NYPD, without the knowledge of local law enforcement, monitored mosques, schools, businesses, and Muslim student groups at public universities. Although it acknowledged no wrongdoing, the NYPD has promised to no longer engage in surveillance on the basis of religion or ethnicity.

Later in 2018, another lawsuit revealed a similar operation in Los Angeles, where the LAPD created a short-lived Muslim community mapping program in 2007. The program was intended to document where in the city there were concentrations of Muslim residents and where Muslims ate, shopped, prayed, and went to school.

Programs like these had—and I would argue continue to have—a chilling effect. They make people question whether they can trust those who are meant to protect them. Perhaps you can imagine that this affects people's capacity to be full citizens, to decide when, where, how, and why to engage in the stuff of public life.

Plaintiffs in the NYPD lawsuit reported that learning about the surveillance program had a real effect on the way they lived their public lives.[6] Some noted that they became afraid to speak about politics in public or in their mosques. One plaintiff, Syed Farhaj Hassan, a sergeant in the Army reserves, stopped worshipping at mosques because he worried that it would damage his reputation.

There are many other accounts of the effects that surveillance has had on people. In *How Does It Feel to Be a Problem*, first published in 2008, Moustafa Bayoumi relates the story of Sade, a young Brooklyn man. In Bayoumi's telling, Sade is upset because he has recently found out that his friend of four years, who disappeared without a trace, was actually an undercover police officer, presumably with the NYPD intelligence bureau. Sade had never been in trouble or associated with criminal activity. He was Muslim—that seemed to be enough to cast him as suspicious.

It's not all that surprising that Sade talks about trusting only those people with whom he has longstanding, familial ties. Wondering who is watching, what they are looking for, and whether you have done something, anything, that could bring on even more attention from law enforcement are not conditions in which people can fully, actively engage in our collective life.

The NYPD and LAPD Muslim surveillance and monitoring programs ended up being discredited, both because they didn't produce any results and because they so clearly stepped over the bounds of what is acceptable for the government to do. They still very much left their mark, showing that government suspicion and surveillance of Muslim communities in the United States had become a significant feature of public life for American Muslims after September 11.

* * *

National political discourse complicates the post–September 11 picture. The George W. Bush administration immediately sought to separate Islam and American Muslims from those responsible for the attacks. President Bush himself visited the Islamic Center of Washington, DC, famously declaring that "Islam is peace." The attacks, he said, "violate the fundamental tenets of the Islamic faith. And it's important for my fellow Americans to understand that."

Later in his remarks, Bush tried to situate Muslims in the fabric of American life. "America counts millions of Muslims amongst our citizens, and Muslims make an incredibly valuable contribution to our country. Muslims are doctors, lawyers, law professors, members of the military, entrepreneurs, shopkeepers, moms and dads. And they need to be treated with respect. In our anger and emotion, our fellow Americans must treat each other with respect."

Bush's comments were part of a larger push by the White House. Other members of the administration made a point of reaching out to and meeting with representatives of American Muslim communities, including Secretary of State Colin Powell and Attorney General John Ashcroft. Mazammil H. Siddiqi, an imam and Muslim scholar, was among those invited to speak at a memorial service at the National Cathedral in Washington, DC, on September 14, 2001.

White House efforts to connect with American Muslim organizations and leaders is not terribly surprising. Nearly three-quarters of American Muslim voters supported Bush's run for the presidency. In retrospect, though, these efforts sit uneasily beside what the federal government and municipal law enforcement agencies were actually doing. This included the detention of many American Muslims and Muslim foreign nationals living legally in the United States immediately after the attacks, the over eight thousand "voluntary" interviews the FBI conducted in the months after September 11 with people on valid visas from countries in the Middle East, and a range of ongoing surveillance programs.

It's also important to remember that planning for war was very much in full swing in the weeks following the attacks. Military engagement in Afghanistan, whose government was hosting Osama bin Laden and al-Qa'ida, began in October of that same year and continued throughout the period under consideration.

What we can see here is a real tension. We have the reality of major cultural trauma brought on by horrific events, leading to actions taken by government at various levels that certainly seemed to suggest that Muslims living in the United States—whether born here or not—were suspect. At the same time, the president of the United States was working hard to convince people that this was not the case, that real Muslims were not to blame.

Officials from the Department of Justice continued to maintain that ethnic and racial profiling was not an acceptable tactic in its efforts to prevent another attack. At the same time, federal law enforcement was engaging in what looked an awful lot like racial profiling.

This same tension was also playing out in public discourse and popular culture, from TV shows and movies to political cartoons and newspaper columns.[7] Many people recognized that profiling people on the basis of race or ethnicity was wrong. People's background or heritage are not good predictors of future behavior. But many people also thought that the attacks of September 11 might very well justify an exception to this rule.

Writing in the *Washington Post*, columnist Richard Cohen captured the national mood regarding the civil rights of Muslims in America. In an opinion piece, "Profiles in Evasiveness," that appeared less than a month after the attacks, Cohen acknowledges the manifold problems with perceptions around race and stereotyping in the United States and then proceeds to defend racial profiling of Arabs. Doing any different would make us "driveling idiots" in the face of an imminent danger, he says.

A quick look at Cohen's other writing makes his pro-profiling stance a little surprising. But this is a good reflection of public discourse in the United States in that pitched moment.

Writing in the same publication just a few days before Cohen, Michael Kinsley, a well-known liberal pundit and journalist, makes a similar case in "When Is Racial Profiling Okay?" He acknowledges that racial profiling is bad, but argues that in this instance reason dictates that we make an exception. What follows from that is rather disturbing.

After voicing some skepticism about the value of increased screening procedures at airports, he says of profiling Arabs, "But assuming these procedures do work, it's hard to argue that helping to avoid another September 11 is not worth the imposition, which is pretty small: inconvenience and embarrassment." He continues,

> A colleague says that people singled out at airport security should be consoled with frequent flier miles. They're already getting an even better consolation: The huge increase in public sensitivity to anti-Muslim and anti-Arab prejudice, which President Bush—to his enormous credit—has made such a focal point of his response to September 11. And many victims of racial profiling at the airport might not need any consolation. After all, they don't want to be hijacked and blown up either.

Two columnists from the *Washington Post* certainly don't prove anything about the immediate post–September 11 environment and the years that followed. But I thought it was worth quoting Kinsley at length because his sentiment represents the ambivalence and tensions that I describe above, capturing the mood of the time: Even many people who otherwise would oppose ethnic and racial profiling thought that it would be wise to make an exception for Muslims.

Kinsley's words point to questions about public space, public life, and what it means to be a full citizen that we've been exploring. He was writing in the immediate wake of horrifying events, and while he may be inadvertently pointing to something that is true—that American Muslims were just as scared by the prospect of another attacks—the leap he takes to imagining that Muslims may not mind being racially profiled just doesn't follow. No one objects to reasonable security procedures. Racial profiling, though, violates the basic premise of equal protection under the law, which is crucial for people to have a basic sense of security in shared public space.

Fundamental American values like equal protection should never be far from our minds as we explore the conditions of public life for American Muslims after September 11, 2001.

The tensions between the idea of equality before the law and the trauma of September 11 that showed up in the words and deeds of the government and in public discourse raise complicated questions for our consideration. Are there exceptions when it comes to the rights we (as a country) afford to citizens or to people living legally in the United States? Who is in a position to decide? On what basis?

The years following the trauma of September 11 saw the emergence of new norms in public life that guided how many Americans thought about such questions. The attacks left people wondering when the next attack might come. Ways of thinking and talking about Islam that might not have been acceptable before September 11 gained normalcy.

It certainly isn't true that all discourses about Islam and Muslims in the months and years after September 11 were completely negative. We can see that the Bush administration really did try to make a nuanced argument. Similar efforts played out in popular culture.

This is the nature of ambivalence. Along with positive statements about the essentially peaceful nature of real Islam and the contributions of real Muslims to American society, the federal government engaged in activities targeting Muslims in the United States that seemed to contradict these sentiments. Commentators who know that racial profiling is inconsistent with American values argued for an exception for Muslims. At times, I wonder how much of this ambivalence was a reflection of how people thought they *ought* to be responding to the situation versus how they *wanted* to respond.

We can't know for sure, of course. But government policies and activities, at national and local levels, when set alongside contributions to public discourse by people like Michael Kinsley, suggest a fairly broad acceptance of the idea that it was okay to make exceptions when it came to the rights of American Muslims.

Perhaps some of you, as you've been reading, find yourselves thinking that this ambivalence makes complete sense. Maybe you find yourself agreeing with *Washington Post* columnist Richard Cohen's defense of racial profiling. In the piece quoted above he says, "One hundred percent of the terrorists involved in the September 11 mass murder were Arabs. Their accomplices, if any, were probably Arabs, too—at least Muslims. Ethnicity and religion are the very basis of their movement."

In his view, not even having a frank discussion of the possible merits of racial profiling after the attacks would be a victory for "a virulent form of political correctness." There are truths in what he said. The perpetrators of the September 11 attacks were Arab and they identified as Muslim. But there's much more to unpack here.

Not all Arabs are Muslim. Not all Muslims are Arab. This simple point highlights the shortcomings of security policies based on racial profiling. Depending on names or eye tests—whether someone "looks Muslim"—to make security decisions guarantees that members of vulnerable communities will receive unequal treatment because of the way that stereotyping works. Security based on racial profiling may make some people feel safer, but only at the expense of making other people afraid. This is not equal protection.

The suspicion of Muslims that became a new norm after the trauma of September 11 affected how many Americans may have thought about whose citizenship, whose rights, are subject to question and in what circumstances. This new norm showed itself in a range of policies and government activities. It also played out in people's everyday lives in other ways.

A Different Kind of Fear

On September 15, 2001, Blabir Singh Sodhi was working with a landscaper in front of his Chevron gas station in Mesa, Arizona. The two men were looking at a broken sprinkler and discussing the flowers that were to be planted. Just then, Frank Roque drove by the gas station and, seeing Sodhi's turban, opened fire from his truck. Sodhi did not survive the attack.

Roque then went on to fire shots into a business where he knew a Lebanese American man was working and into the home he had sold to an Afghani family. When police apprehended him he shouted, "I stand for America all the way! I'm an American. Go ahead. Arrest me and let those terrorists run wild!" Sodhi, a Sikh American, was likely the first fatality in response to the September 11 attacks.

Less than a week later, Rais Bhuiyan was working in a Dallas-area gas station when a man named Mark Stroman walked in. Stroman looked at Bhuiyan and asked, "Where are you from?" He did not give Bhuiyan the chance to answer. He raised his gun and shot him in the face. Although there was no coverage of the shooting at the time, Stroman's involvement in the case eventually came to light when he was apprehended in the October 2001 killing of Vasudev Patel.

Bhuiyam was the lone survivor of a violent spree targeting Muslims, or people Stroman assumed were Muslim, after September 11. In addition to the Patel and Bhuiyan shootings, authorities charged Stroman in the murder of Waqar Hasan. This appears to have been his first attack. As Stroman confessed, he killed Hasan on September 14, 2001.

Stroman is very clear about what motivated him. He described the attacks as a patriotic response to terrorism. He wanted to punish people from the Middle East. None of his three targets were from the Middle East. Only two were Muslim. But this is precisely why it's so important to consider anti-Muslim hostility in the context of broader histories of people of color in the United States. Stroman was using racial profiling as the basis of his attacks.

Like Roque, Stroman believed he was defending the United States. "We're at war," he said. "I did what I had to do." He is thought to have said "God bless America" just before he shot Patel. Stroman further described his motives in media interviews.

"I did what every American wanted to but didn't. They didn't have the nerve."

Stroman admitted that when police apprehended him, with weapons in his vehicle, he was on his way to attack a Dallas-area mosque. "I was going to go in shooting Arabs."

* * *

Stroman's claim that he was merely doing what every other American *really* wanted to is obviously mistaken. But. Hate crimes against Muslims did surge immediately after the September 11 attacks. FBI statistics show that there were 481 anti-Muslim hate crimes over the remainder of the year, up from 28 the entire previous year.

In terms of percentages, the increase in anti-Muslim hate crimes is staggering: 1,617 percent. It's also very important to remember that even by the FBI's own accounting, hate crime statistics are not very reliable. According to the Bureau of Justice Statistics, which gathers data through residential surveys instead of relying on voluntary reporting by law enforcement agencies, as the FBI does, hate crime statistics significantly underrepresent what people are actually experiencing.

Given the traumatic nature of the September 11 attacks, some commentators didn't think that the spike in hate crimes was all that bad. Take, for example, veteran reporter Dillon Gallow.

Writing in the *Orange County Register* about Orange County, California, which experienced one of the sharpest increases in hate crimes in the country following the September 11 attacks, Gallow suggests that government officials and the media were exaggerating the problem. After calling for those perpetrating hate crimes to be punished, Gallow says, "But I wish the attorney general—and the news media—would see that, based on the numbers, the real news about hate crimes in California and in Orange County isn't that there are so many of them. No, the real news, the good news, is that relatively speaking, there are so few."

We really don't know how much anti-Muslim hate crimes increased immediately after September 11. We do have some data, but it's pretty flawed. According to National Archive of Criminal Justice data, we have information from only twenty-one states for 2001. Just as important to consider is that given the environment at the time it would not be at all surprising if many people who were attacked opted to avoid law enforcement altogether.

Beyond questions about data, though, there is something else for us to think about when it comes to the effects that hate crimes have on communities of people.

Above, we discussed the idea of cultural trauma as a concept that can help us make sense of the effect that the September 11 attacks had on people across the United States, not just those who directly experienced them. Let's think for a moment about where American Muslims fit into this picture.

Like other Americans, they experienced the shock of the horrific events. Muslims in the United States were especially horrified once news broke that nineteen Muslims, claiming to act in the name of Islam, were responsible. They were also experiencing a general climate of anti-Muslim sentiment, including an immediate increase in hate crimes and the official suspicion that motivated policymakers following September 11.

A 2018 article in the *Express-Times*, a Pennsylvania newspaper, takes us back to that moment. Writing as the seventeenth anniversary of September 11 approached, a man named Mohammed Khaku shares how he felt in the months after the attacks. "First, I had experienced an attack by an extremist group on our country by individuals who committed this criminal act of violence in the name of Islam. Second, during the tumultuous days after September 11, 2001, American Muslims, including myself, not only were mourning this tragic event but had to deal with a backlash of anti-Muslim sentiments and hate crimes that continue to today."

I want to spend a moment thinking about what I'll call Mohammad Khaku's "double trauma." He shared with many other Americans the trauma of the events themselves. At the same time, he was also becoming acutely aware of the suspicion with which others were seeing Muslims and the ways that was playing out in public life.

Khaku doesn't describe having been the target of a hate crime himself. But we don't have to directly experience something for it to have a very real effect on our lives. The September 11 attacks are certainly a case in point. A relatively small number of Americans had connections to those directly affected. Most people experienced the attacks by following news coverage. And yet they, too, were profoundly affected by the events that day even without directly experiencing them. It would make sense that American Muslim experience of the rise in hate crimes after September 11 would follow the same logic.

A quick search of media coverage of anti-Muslim hate crimes shows that from September 11, 2001, through the end of January 2002 there were over two thousand articles written about the rise in anti-Muslim hate crimes, to say nothing of other forms of media. By the end of September, FBI director Robert Mueller reported that thirty FBI field offices were investigating attacks against Arabs, Muslims, and Sikhs. Word of such investigations would certainly travel through community circles.

One article, written by Richard Serrano for the *Los Angeles Times* in late September, reflects the moment. In addition to FBI investigations, he reports, "local police and state agencies are handling hundreds of other hate-related cases, including slayings in San Gabriel, Dallas, and Mesa, Arizona, as well as numerous shootings, beatings and incidents in which individuals have been dragged from their cars."

There is no question that these crimes, along with others that Serrano did not include, such as vandalism of mosques and businesses, combined with the more general climate of suspicion to create an environment of fear for American Muslims and other communities whose members were affected by anti-Muslim activities. Not every individual needed to experience something directly for the increase in hate-related activity to affect them.[8]

Reshma Memon Yaqub, a well-established essayist, published a commentary on September 13, 2001, that illustrates this point. In the piece, which appeared in newspapers across the country, she said,

Like every American, I am outraged. And I want justice. But perhaps unlike many other Americans, I'm feeling something else, too. A different kind of fear. I'm feeling what my 6 million fellow American Muslims are feeling—the fear that we too will be considered guilty in the eyes of America, if it turns out that the madmen behind this terrorism were Muslims.

She continued,

I feel as though I've suddenly become the enemy of two groups—those who wish to hurt Americans, and those Americans who wish to strike back. It's a frightening corner to be in.

Yaqub was someone with reputation enough to make it possible for her to publish an opinion piece in major media outlets. She used this relative privilege to communicate something that American Muslims across the country were feeling. Reshma had not directly experienced the September 11 attacks, nor had she been target of a hate crime. Yet she was experiencing the same kind of two-pronged fear that Mohammed Khaku described—one part growing out of a trauma felt by all Americans, the other out of the particular experiences of American Muslims.

A few days after the publication of her piece, Reshma Yaqub appeared on a two-hour-long televised program on C-SPAN, the public service station, about Arab and Muslim American experiences of the September 11 attacks and their aftermath. One of the things that struck me about the many guests who appeared, a "who's who" of Arab and Muslim America at the time, is the lengths they went to highlight their Americanness.

Like everyone else, they, too, were scared that there would be more attacks. But they also faced the weight of knowing that so many people were suspicious of them. In some situations, this suspicion led to real violence, like the cases that I talked about at the beginning of this section. While these may be on the extreme end, suspicion also showed itself in smaller ways that nonetheless had real effects across Muslim communities.

On the television program, Yaqub told a couple of stories that people had related to her. One woman was forbidden entry onto a public bus by the driver, who told her, "This bus isn't going where you need to go." Another woman was refused service at a grocery store, where an employee said, "We aren't selling you our food."

These kinds of experiences don't rise to the level of murder and assault. But this should not lead us to downplay their significance, in part because they are rarely isolated incidents. They are the moments that accumulate over time to make people feel like they don't belong, like they don't have the same access to public space as others.

Anti-Muslim hate crimes decreased and leveled off by early 2002. Statistics show that for the remainder of the decade after 2001 the number of reported hate crimes targeting Muslims hovered somewhere between 100 and 160 per year. This is a remarkable decrease, even if the annual figures were still higher than before 2001. But this doesn't mean that the tremendous rise in anti-Muslim sentiment, and the kind of public ambivalence described above, simply went away.

When they accumulate over time, small moments of indignity like those Yaqub describes, along with direct experience or knowledge of hate crimes, policies targeting Muslims, and a general climate of suspicion, can create what sociologist and legal scholar Angela Onwuachi-Willig calls an expectation of routine harm. For vulnerable communities, community or cultural trauma can result from extended experiences of discrimination by government agencies and fellow citizens. The result is that people begin to expect that because of who they are they will encounter something scary, hurtful, or dangerous as they move through their everyday lives.

Leila Fadel, a reporter for National Public Radio, once referred to the "ongoing trauma" of being Muslim in the United States.[9] The memories of the dramatic rise in anti-Muslim hate crimes and anti-Muslim sentiment in the months after September 11, 2001, were not so faded a decade later that what we began seeing in 2010 with the rehabilitation of public hate didn't connect back to those experiences in deepening, or at least reigniting, an expectation of routine harm.

The kind of fear that Maheen Haq described in her op-ed didn't come out of nowhere for American Muslims. There is deep community memory among Muslims in the United States of the immediate aftermaths of September 11. Nor, for that matter, did the fear of Islam and Muslims that anti-Muslim activists have successfully nurtured in the years since 2010 come out of nowhere. The country's memory of September 11 is deep as well.

The question, as I've noted before, is what we do with that fear, whom we listen to, and where that takes us in our public lives.

* * *

Criminal justice experts Bryan D. Byers and James A. Jones argue that the marked decrease in anti-Muslim hate crimes after the initial post–September 11 spike was at least in part due to public calls for calm and tolerance, including those from Muslim advocacy organizations and the White House.[10]

We shouldn't discount the positive effects of these public efforts or more private instances of people reaching out to Muslim communities to voice support in the days, weeks, months, and years after September 11. There are, to be sure, many heartwarming stories.

Reshma Yaqub made a point of mentioning such instances of support during her September 18, 2001, television appearance. She and the program host briefly exchanged stories.

Yaqub says, "I've been heartened by some very positive responses I've gotten."

The host, who is also Muslim, interjects, "Yes, I've been getting emails. Beautiful friends calling."

Yaqub continues, "A head of a church called me and said, 'Can we come and scrub graffiti off your mosque?' If people are feeling that way and if they want to reach out, I hope they will because it means a lot."

It's important to note that while such gestures mean a lot, Yaqub never says that they made her less fearful. Still, they suggest that in 2001 there was a possible path forward, cleared by non-Muslim Americans as well as efforts of American Muslims themselves. This path might have led to American Muslim experiences of suspicion and a sense of "double trauma" fading with time. Similarly, it might have yielded the kinds of connections that would prevent fear of Muslims from taking hold. Many non-Muslim Americans have in fact traveled down this path in the years since 2001. However, at the same time, others were preparing an alternate way forward, a path that has led to a very different place.

This is the path of fear and public hate that you've been reading about through much of this book. It's one of the aftermaths of September 11. It's not the only aftermath, however. The question before us is which aftermath we choose to carry forward in our public lives.

Anti-Muslim hostility and activity haven't prevented American Muslims from engaging in public life, as we will see in the next chapter. Anti-Muslim sentiment and activity appear to have required particular kinds of engagement—and created the conditions for a compelling, if not fraught, story of resiliency in the face of fear. This story is also an aftermath of September 11.

5

Humanizing Public Life

Fear plays an outsized role in our collective public life. Nurtured by anti-Muslim activists, fear of Muslims has led to a wide variety of anti-Muslim activity. It's spurred legislation and other policies that purposefully treat American Muslims differently from other citizens and residents of the United States. It's led to higher and higher levels of harassment, discrimination, vandalism, violent threats, and violence targeting Muslims.

These conditions of public life have in turn generated fear *for* American Muslims. In the first chapter, Maheen Haq described it as fear in her heart. American Muslim responses to the conditions of their public lives offer a path of public life for us all to consider moving forward. It is a path that leads us toward a humane public life. It's a fraught path because it has taken shape in the midst of vulnerable communities' fears. But it's a path nonetheless that can lead us to a public life together that is more in line with what the vast majority of Americans declared in a 2018 poll (see the introduction) as the core of what it means to be of this country: to treat people equally.

Two stories, set side by side, will help us begin to explore this path and the small steps it encourages us all to take.

Samer's Story

In November 2015, Samer Shalaby stood before a packed room in Fredericksburg, Virginia. He was at a public planning meeting, representing the Islamic Center of Fredericksburg, whose members were seeking to build a new mosque to replace one that had served area Muslims for over thirty years. When we enter the scene, things are more or less moving along as you might expect at this kind of meeting. Storm drains. Sewage removal. Traffic. Parking spots. And then things quickly change.

One member of the audience asks a question about parking spots. Would forty be enough to accommodate all the worshippers?

"That's forty too many," one audience member says, first softly and then louder, with more confidence.

There is a murmur in the crowd.

"Let me tell you something," he continues. "Nobody. Nobody. Nobody wants your evil cult in this town."

Some people voice obvious displeasure at where this is heading. Other people clap and encourage him to continue, which he does.

"I will do everything in my power to make sure that does not happen."

Another voice chimes in, "We don't want it." Others clap.

"Because you are terrorists. Every one of you are terrorists. I don't care what you say. I don't care what you think."

Samer meets the outburst with a bemused, nonthreatening expression as some others continue to clap.

"You can smile at me. You can say anything you want. Every Muslim is a terrorist. Period."

Samer begins to speak in a calm manner.

"Shut your mouth. I don't want to hear your mouth. I'm done with you. Everything that I will do, everything I can do, to keep you from doing what you are doing, will happen. That will happen."

Law enforcement officers ended the meeting after the audience member walked out.

It's not necessarily unusual that a planning meeting turns contentious. But this incident is of a different nature than disagreements about stop signs, traffic lights, or run-of-the-mill building permits.

What the audience member said to Samer is, sadly, not all that surprising. What is surprising, though, is that the audience member felt so free to speak publicly in this way. Aside from murmurs of dissent, no one intervened. No one shouted down the audience member.

A planning meeting like this one exemplifies local public life. The fact that the audience member was able to accuse Samer of being a terrorist without any apparent repercussions—in fact, with open support from some other audience members—reflects the conditions of public life in our country. It's pretty easy to imagine how such an encounter in public space could leave someone with questions about whether they are full citizens.

The familiarity on display in the meeting is striking.[1] People refer to each other by first name. The proposal under discussion is clearly part of an ongoing discussion. After all, the Islamic Center of Fredericksburg has been around for over three decades with no incident. The Shalaby family has been a part of the community for almost as long and, as a trustee of the Center, I am sure Samer has been in front of that same room many times before. The whole incident just doesn't add up.

There is a disjuncture between the familiarity that comes from shared histories and experiences in local communities and the kind of hostility on display in this meeting. It seems that for the hostile audience member and those who encouraged him Samer was just a stand-in for a larger, more abstract group. "Every one of you are terrorists."

Mohammad's Story

On Monday, February 26, 2017, Mohammad Qamar stepped up to the podium at a meeting of the Downtown Rotary Club in Sioux Falls, South Dakota. He'd been invited to address the civic organization as the director of his mosque's public outreach and interfaith initiatives.

After introducing himself—and noting that he has two kids, both of whom were born in the United States—he says, "I have a confession to make. I've been doing talks such as this, visiting churches over the past year, hosting different groups at our center. But I would much rather not have to do this." And yet he's there, which he says "is not just important. It is a necessity."

Dr. Qamar, a nephrologist, arrived in the United States in 2004. He is a member of South Dakota Faith and Public Life, which describes itself as a group of religious leaders committed to respectful discussion of difficult social and political issues. His deep engagement with public life is clear. Now here he finds himself giving a talk that I'm sure he has delivered many times over. He spends a lot of time describing why.

Sometimes he uses humor to do so, noting, for example, that while approval ratings of Muslims are going up, they still are competing with pretty much only zombies at the low end of the scale. Most of the time, though, he is serious. He notes that the number of anti-Muslim hate groups increased from four in 2010 to over one hundred in 2016. He discusses the fact that nearly six in ten Americans report not knowing anyone who is Muslim.

He has taken on the burden of speaking to audiences in Sioux Falls so that in his city, at least, that figure will decrease. He is humanizing himself so that Muslims don't remain an undifferentiated other. He wants his audience to feel like they know him and that he fundamentally shares their values.

He talks about his first visit to the United States, which happened to coincide with the September 11 attacks, to illustrate this point. He talks about being terrified, of wanting to return to Pakistan as soon as he could. But what he found surprised him. He describes feeling like President Bush was speaking directly to him when he offered reassuring words that Islam was a religion of peace. Although he was aware of anti-Muslim activity occurring across the country in the wake of the attacks, he describes experiencing tremendous kindness from those around him.

He decided then and there that he wanted to make the United States his home.

* * *

It's hard to move past the idea that Dr. Qamar thinks outreach of the kind he does "is not just important. It is a necessity."

During his talk, he says that he and the other three thousand or so Muslims in Sioux Falls have decided to make the small city their home because they feel comfortable. They feel certain that, despite the conditions of public life nationally, they and their kids can move through their everyday lives in Sioux Falls without serious, immediate threat.

Yet his mosque has an entire center devoted to public outreach, which, despite having a demanding professional life and kids at home, he directs. He also clearly spends a lot of time preparing and giving talks to audiences like Rotary. Why?

Demanding a Response

Together, the stories about Samer Shalaby and Mohammad Qamar present in microcosm the ideas we are exploring in this whole book. The anti-Muslim sentiment on display during Samer Shalaby's town planning meeting presentation exemplifies the conditions of public life that have emerged with the rehabilitation of public hate. Mohammad Qamar's talk at the Rotary club helps turn our attention to how American Muslims have responded to these conditions in showing how and why they are part of this country.

Read side by side, these stories highlight the fact that both anti-Muslim sentiment and American Muslim participation in public life aren't always simply reflections of direct experiences that people have. We draw on things we see on TV, read on social media or in magazines or books, and hear from friends near and far. These indirect experiences also inform the paths we take in our public lives.

It's unlikely that many people clapping in the audience at the 2015 planning meeting in Fredericksburg had direct experience supporting the claim that every Muslim is a terrorist. Still, their clapping and encouragement suggested that they had traveled far down a certain path guiding their participation in public life in that moment. This path was cleared by people seeking to rehabilitate public hate, taking a fact—that there are a small number of Muslims in the world who do awful things—and distorting it into terrible generalizations about millions of people.

For his part, Dr. Qamar stood before the Downtown Rotary Club in Sioux Falls because others around the country had been so successful in paving this path of public hate, not because of a particular history of anti-Muslim activity in the city. In response, he was following, and helping to further build, another path of public life, one built on the idea that humanization—the simple idea of reminding others of our common humanity—makes it harder to hate.

The paths we select as we decide how, when, where, and why to engage in public life typically reflect our local settings. Yet these settings, and thus our decisions related to public life, are always tied into larger networks. Studying anti-Muslim sentiment and activity shows in very real terms that the conditions of public life come from the complex interaction of local and national factors.

This national-local dynamic explains how something like anti-Muslim sentiment and activity exists in very different places across the country—towns and cities with and without Muslim communities, towns and cities that have and have not experienced violence perpetrated by Muslims. It also explains how American Muslim responses to anti-Muslim sentiment and activity have unfolded across the country.

Reading these stories side by side also highlights the close relationship between anti-Muslim sentiment and the humanizing work of American Muslims. It's not really possible to understand the remarkable growth of outreach efforts undertaken by everyday American Muslims across the country—like Dr. Qamar in Sioux Falls—without considering the rise of anti-Muslim sentiment and activity like we saw in Fredericksburg.[2]

These hostile conditions in effect create a need—even a requirement—for American Muslims to engage in public life in particular kinds of ways. Their own fear, they own expectations of routine harm, have created the need to minister to *others'* fears. This has led to an unprecedented, largely organic, outreach and public engagement effort by American Muslim communities.

Humanizing outreach comes in many different shapes and sizes. The goal, whatever the form, is always the same: humanizing Muslims in the face of anti-Muslim sentiment that assumes that all Muslims are the same (bad, in a nutshell).

An April 2018 mosque open house event in Roxbury, Massachusetts, captures the spirit of this kind of work. The event featured tours of the mosque, mini classes about Islam, opportunities to learn about Arabic calligraphy, and an afternoon prayer that visitors could observe. Above all else, the open house provided opportunities for people of all ages to talk together. Speaking to the *Boston Globe*, Yusufi Vali, one of the organizers, said of the event, "The real benefit of this is people get to meet real people and make their own judgments about who Muslims are."

By embarking on an incredibly ambitious humanization effort in the face of rising anti-Muslim sentiment, Muslim communities and individuals have worked hard to create a path for others to follow when fear descends on public life. Many non-Muslims have certainly supported them in this work, but the resiliency American Muslims have shown in responding to anti-Muslim sentiment and activity is really quite remarkable.

In many of the media reports I've read, people doing this humanizing work have expressed joy at the connections their outreach has made possible. Just because they enjoy the work, though, doesn't mean that the conditions of public life have left them with much choice about doing the work in the first place. Are Americans like Samer Shalaby and Mohammad Qamar really free to choose how they engage in public life? The answer to this question, at least as I've come to think about it in researching and writing this book, troubles me.

During the question-and-answer session of Dr. Qamar's talk, one member of the audience asked him where they could find moderate Muslim voices denouncing extremism. This request is a common variation on the general theme of collective responsibility, an idea which we'll discuss a little more below. In response, Dr. Qamar provided a number of resources and issued an open invitation for everyone to visit his mosque and ask any questions they had about Islam.

I'm not sure the person who asked the question recognized that Dr. Qamar was a living, breathing answer to the question—or perhaps he just thought that Dr. Qamar was an exception.

No matter how misguided it may be, the commonness of the audience member's question is precisely why Dr. Qamar thinks it's "not just important," but "a necessity" to give talks like the one at the Downtown Rotary Club. He and others trying to humanize Muslims to non-Muslim audiences are doing so because of assumptions that all Muslims are responsible for the bad things that other Muslims do.

These assumptions, as well as the conditions of public life for American Muslims in general, in effect demand a response from Muslim communities—an accounting of why all Muslims should not be subject to suspicion.

As has been clearly noted in our discussions above, there are Muslims, or people identifying as Muslim, who do terrible things. The same is also true for virtually every other conceivable group of people. Yet there is a particular demand on Muslims for a collective response, and it comes in different forms. The question posed to Dr. Qamar is an example of an explicit demand for a response. The planning meeting in Fredericksburg is an example of an implicit, but no less pressing, kind of demand.

For a community made insecure by anti-Muslim sentiment and activity around the country, demands by others *require* a response. For the thousands and thousands of people engaging in these efforts over many years, the requirement for humanizing work has meant less time with family, less time building careers, and less time participating in public life in other ways. In very important respects this was not truly a form of voluntary participation in public life, which is a crucial element of life in a democratic system.

This chapter explores the resiliency and creativity with which American Muslims, like Dr. Qamar and so many others, have nonetheless responded to these demands as they try to humanize the conditions of Muslim public life. As they have gone about this very difficult—even if sometimes joyful—task, American Muslims have provided a model of public life that looks at fear head on and chooses a different path, a path of openness and welcome.

Responding to a Demand

From the beginning of 2010 through the end of 2018, there were over fifteen hundred media reports of American Muslim communities engaging in humanizing work. My data does not capture every instance of humanizing work. It's limited by what receives media coverage. Even then, there's a good chance that I've missed some. Still, I'm confident that what I've collected can help identify important trends and introduce some amazing Americans who are doing this work.

To help make sense of what I've found, I've developed some categories to organize the different kind of activities through which American Muslims have tried to humanize Muslims' presence in public life. What unites them all is a desire to develop connections with non-Muslims.

One category of such efforts is interfaith work. Sometimes this means that Muslims participate in interfaith work hosted by others. Sometimes Muslim communities host programs, inviting others to join. A second category covers a range of activities that I call public outreach. This includes, though is not limited to, open mosque events, where a community invites people to meet and chat with members of the congregation, have a mosque tour, observe prayer, and perhaps share a meal; "Ask a Muslim" and "Meet a Muslim" programming; and fair-style events with a variety of booths that might include Muslims answering questions, introducing people to cultural practices such as henna tattooing and headscarf styles, and offering different kinds of food.

The boundaries between these categories are admittedly blurry. I found that events often have different elements that could have led me to categorize them in different ways. In general, I try to get a sense of how organizers talk about their goals and categorized them accordingly.

Not surprisingly, the rates of interfaith and outreach work over this period reflect the broader conditions of public life. In 2010, just as the Park51 controversy was heating up, humanizing work increased significantly. Of the 167 reports of interfaith and various kinds of outreach work during the year, 131 came in its final five months, 106 in August, September, and October alone.

A number of the reports about humanizing work during this period make the connection to the Park51 controversy and the associated rise in anti-Muslim activity very clear.

On September 3, for example, Masjid Saad, a mosque in Sylvania, Ohio, hosted an interfaith prayer vigil. Speaking to the *Toledo Blade*, one of the event organizers, Salmenna Sediqe, said, "Unfortunately, during the holy month of Ramadan [which went from early August through early September that year], we experienced—not in Toledo, but nationwide—many anti-Muslim activities." Salmenna, who was the first woman to be elected president of the mosque, mentioned a number of developments she had in mind: opposition to Park51; threats made against a mosque in Murfreesboro, Tennessee, then still in the planning stages; and an incident, which we previously encountered, in which a young man named Michael Enright attacked and stabbed a cab driver after asking him if he was Muslim.

A couple of weeks earlier, in mid-August, a group of mosques and community centers in the Bay Area of Northern California coordinated a series of open houses. Speaking to the *Mercury News*, Jason van Boom, who helped organize an open house at the Islamic Cultural Center of North California, said, "Our open house is a way of welcoming and introducing ourselves to our neighbors. It's a day for us to reach out." The event, he continued, was a way to address the "mistaken mystique about Islamic centers" that some people have.

Zahra Billoo, who helped coordinate the open-house series, echoed van Boom's thoughts in explaining the wide participation of mosques in the area. "This year there was an increase of interest, an increase of enthusiasm because of all the opposition to mosques that's been happening across the country."

Similarly, Tariq Rasheed, imam and director of the Islamic Center of Orlando, who helped organize a late-August interfaith iftar, or dinner during Ramadan to break the day-long fast, said to the *Orlando Sentinel*, "This past year there's been growing Islamophobia spreading in the US. We felt we had to show the real faith of Islam to the people. They need to know who we are. Everybody is not Osama bin Laden."

Bill Barnes, pastor of St. Luke's United Methodist Church in Orlando, agreed. He said, "to be supportive of our Muslim friends is an important value for us" in such pitched times. Two dozen or so members of his congregation were helping to build and maintain a path to counter the rehabilitation of public hate underway at that time. The importance of non-Muslims standing by Muslim members of local communities, especially in times of duress, comes up frequently in the many reports I've read.

After 2010, there seems to have been an effort by Muslim communities to find allies in as broad a cross-section of the public as possible. I found more reports of general public outreach than reports of interfaith work in the years from 2011 to 2014. Overall, outreach work appeared to slow down somewhat from 2012 to 2014, with the number of total reports each year coming in lower than in 2010 and 2011. This changed in 2015.

In a year that saw a tremendous rise in anti-Muslim activity, especially toward the end of the year, Muslim communities in the United States also significantly increased their outreach efforts. There are more than double the number of recorded efforts in 2015 than in 2014. Not surprisingly, this increase coincided almost exactly with the jump in anti-Muslim sentiment and activity that came toward the end of the year. There were 78 reports of interfaith events and other forms of public outreach in November and December alone.

Interfaith work and other forms of outreach increased significantly from 2015 to 2017. In 2015, there were 143 documented outreach events.

In 2016, there were 151, and in 2017, there were 273. The number decreases in 2018, with 174 reports of interfaith and public outreach work in 2018. These figures track closely with measures of anti-Muslim activity, including my own data as well as hate crime statistics from law enforcement agencies.

Addressing Collective Guilt

The data shows that there is a connection between anti-Muslim activity and the ways that American Muslims engage in public life. This is not about a simple dichotomy between participating in public life or not. We all engage in aspects of public life throughout our everyday lives. The question is whether we have the freedom and ability to decide what that participation looks like—the when, where, why, and how of public life—and to what extent we feel like public space belongs to us.

A few paragraphs above, I mentioned an interfaith prayer vigil that took place just outside Toledo, Ohio, in September 2010. Salmenna Sediqe, one of the event organizers, talked about how the rise in anti-Muslim activity that year was motivating her and her colleagues to reach out to other communities. Of the prayer vigil, she told the *Toledo Blade*, "We hope it's a way to prevent any anti-Muslim activities and also to show that we have the support of other faiths, not just Muslims."

Perhaps this quote makes an obvious point. A community is scared, and so they reach out to others to try and demonstrate that they are part of a broader public. Yet in her comments to the newspaper, Salmenna is very careful to point out that Muslims in Toledo have not directly experienced the rise in anti-Muslim activity. This may or may not be the case given what we know about the everyday nature of much anti-Muslim activity. Still, she is suggesting that the interfaith prayer vigil did not arise because of a particular incident. Something else is going on.

Another of the event organizers made a comment that sheds light on what motivated the organizers. Dr. Zaheer Hasan, a member of the United Muslim Association of Toledo, told the *Toledo Blade*, "Every day, the level of hatred and animosity toward Muslim communities is increasing, and the sad thing is, it's not just focused on terrorism or 9/11, but anything about Muslims is being attacked. Because the September 11 attacks were carried out by so-called Muslims, all Muslims are bearing the brunt and collective guilt is being thrown on us."

Assigning collective guilt for something to a whole group of people (Muslims in this case) creates a staggering demand: Each and every member of that group must answer for things that others, who happen to share one element of their identity, do.[3] Assigning collective guilt and demanding a collective apology doesn't really make much sense—why would we expect an apology from someone on behalf of someone else with whom they have no concrete connection?

Even if it doesn't make much sense, the effect of collective guilt being assigned to an entire community is very real. This is what much of this book has been about.

Contemporary anti-Muslim sentiment and activity is the result of anti-Muslim activists assigning collective guilt to all Muslims for terrible things that a very small number of Muslims have done. This is not to say that the trauma and fear that result from terrorism isn't real or legitimate. It's just not clear what value comes from assigning guilt to an entire group of people as a result.

What is clear is that assigning collective guilt has the effect of creating an ongoing demand. Like Dr. Qamar, who you met at the beginning of this chapter, Muslims in Toledo hoped that by getting out in front of the problem, by demonstrating their peaceful commitment to the greater Toledo community, they could prevent the bad things happening around the country from happening to them. The conditions of public life for American Muslims, suffused with the idea that all Muslims are responsible for all things done in the name of Islam, requires individuals and communities to meet an almost insatiable demand to engage in humanizing public outreach.

American Muslims around the country have spent thousands of hours since 2010 answering this demand. These efforts certainly date back further, beginning after September 11. With the rehabilitation of public hate in 2010, though, their efforts took on even greater urgency. We'll pick up this story in 2015, when demands rooted in the assignment of collective guilt became even more urgent as anti-Muslim sentiment grew and anti-Muslim activity began to become an ever-greater part of public life.

Whining Isn't Going to Help

Charlie Hebdo, the Bataclan, and the Stade de France, all in and around Paris. The Inland Regional Center in San Bernardino, California. These were sites of significant acts of terror in 2015, all with the rise of Daesh, or ISIS, looming large. There was plenty of cause for fear for Americans. Anti-Muslim activists and other public figures set about fanning and nurturing this fear in a variety of ways. Quite predictably, a significant rise in anti-Muslim activity followed—and so did American Muslim efforts to reach out to non-Muslims.

For American Muslims, the fear that understandably arrives for all Americans in the wake of terrorist attacks comes with an added layer of concern about anti-Muslim activity—with good reason.

On November 15, 2015, members of the Baitul Aman mosque in Meriden, New York, arrived to discover bullet holes in the face of the building, some of which had pierced the wall.

On December 4, 2015, Sherif Elhosseiny, president of the Islamic Center of Palm Beach, in Florida, arrived to find that someone had broken into their mosque and had done significant damage, including breaking more than half of the building's windows.

On December 13, 2015, members of the Baitus Salaam mosque in Hawthorn, California, arrived to find that someone had spray painted "Jesus" and crosses across the building and had left a toy grenade inside.

Each of these communities decided that the best response to these acts of hatred and intimidation was to invite people to join them.

The Baitul Aman mosque offered an open invitation to observe Friday services, the equivalent of Saturday services in synagogues and Sunday services in churches, and to have a tour of the mosque. Hamid Malik, the mosque's imam, said that the response from the general community had been very supportive. "This is why we love America," he told the *Hartford Courant.*

In Florida, members of the Islamic Center of Palm Beach hosted an open house for anyone curious to see the mosque, meet a Muslim, and ask questions. According to a report in the *Palm Beach Post*, a visiting imam, Abu Muhammad al-Maghribee, told the assembled guests, "You don't have to be afraid of who we are. We shop in the same mall and have coffee in the same Starbucks. We go to the same Whole Foods. We don't come from another planet." He added, "I don't blame the non-Muslims for having fear."

Speaking to the *Daily Breeze*, Jalaluddin Ahmad, president of the Baitus Salaam mosque in Hawthorn, said of the vandalism at his community's mosque, "Such extremism will not scare us into locking our mosques; rather we will open the doors wider to educate all."

The theme of transparency is common in how these communities responded to the anti-Muslim activity targeting them. Come in. We're like you. We've nothing to hide.

Not all efforts to reach out to non-Muslims—to be transparent in the face of anti-Muslim sentiment—came in the form of open mosque events like these. More and more American Muslims conducted various forms of outreach in different kinds of public spaces, a phenomenon that grew along with rates of anti-Muslim activity in 2016 and 2017.

The Islamic Society of Greenville, South Carolina, for example, led a late-November downtown rally proclaiming their opposition to Daesh (ISIS). Ali Alkelani, who helped organize the event, held a sign that read, "Muslims Against ISIS." He told the *Greenville News* that the rally came in response to people trying to tie all Muslims to ISIS. "This is something we are really against. We believe ISIS is a terrorist organization.

And the Muslims, they have nothing to do with ISIS. So we as Muslims, we oppose the ideology and acts of ISIS. So we're here to say we have nothing to do with ISIS."

Residents of Hamtramck, Michigan, a city that became a popular target of anti-Muslim rhetoric in 2015 after elections that brought a Muslim-majority city council, hosted a similar rally in December.

A woman named Mona Haydar took a slightly different approach to public outreach. On December 18 and 19, 2015, she and her husband stood outside a public library in Cambridge, Massachusetts. Holding doughnuts under signs that read "Talk to a Muslim" and "Ask a Muslim," Mona talked with anyone and everyone who approached, answering all kinds of questions.

Speaking to the *Boston Globe*, she said, "We just wanted to talk to people and we didn't see any harm in doing that. We are just normal people. There is definitely fear [in America], and I want to talk about it, because it's actually misplaced and misguided—I am really nice!"

Mona Haydar's approach to outreach seems to have started a movement of sorts—or at least signaled that a new kind of outreach was emerging: Ask a Muslim and Meet a Muslim events in public spaces. While opportunities to meet Muslims and ask questions about Islam have long been part of outreach efforts, I noticed that more and more events with names like this were occurring outside of mosques and apart from interfaith outreach.

In mid-January 2016, Moina Shaiq, a resident of Fremont, California, decided that something needed to change. She was serving as the president of the Tri-Cities Interfaith Council, an organization that promotes religious tolerance through interfaith events, but she began wondering just how effective such programming can be in the big picture. "That's like preaching to the choir," she said to the *San Jose Mercury News*. "I kept thinking: What can I do to reach ordinary people that never come to these [interfaith] events?"

She decided to place an ad in the local newspaper inviting people to a coffeeshop to meet a Muslim. Over one hundred people showed up to meet her and ask questions, enough to convince her to hold more events, and to eventually begin traveling the country holding Meet a Muslim events. In October 2017, for example, she was invited to hold a Meet a Muslim event in East Arlington, Vermont, a small rural town in which opportunities to meet someone who's Muslim are few and far between.

Kathleen Clark, the local pastor who invited her, said to the *Bennington Banner*, "Moina's really an ordinary woman; she's a mother, a grandmother, and an active member of her community. We hope that the discussion can help to dispel some of the myths or ideas that exist regarding Islam."

Like so many American Muslims who engage in humanizing work, Moina is just an ordinary person—who is doing extraordinary things to humanize Muslims in the face of anti-Muslim sentiment.

Just after her original Meet a Muslim event, she said, "Whining isn't going to help—action is. I'm just trying to make a difference in my own little way that I as a Muslim person can do."

A Burden to Prove Ourselves

Just about at the same time that Moina Shaiq was welcoming people to Suju's Coffee and Tea in Fremont, California, Robert Azzi was speaking in Peterborough, New Hampshire. A photojournalist by trade and a longtime contributor to the *Concord Monitor*, Robert Azzi began appearing around New Hampshire, often in public libraries, to answer any questions that people had about Islam and Muslims. He called the Peterborough event—the first of well over one hundred like it, by his count—"Ask a Muslim Anything."

Like Moina, he answered questions about a huge range of subjects. One audience member asked why more Muslims don't condemn extremism and terrorism. According to a reporter from the *Union Leader*, who was in attendance, Azzi responded by saying that they do—often—but that the media tends not to give this quite as much coverage as the bad stuff. This is exactly how Moina Shaiq answered the same question.

In a lot of ways, they are both living proof of their responses. Media coverage of their work—and humanizing work more generally—tends to appear in local newspapers, whose reach is by nature limited. But this doesn't change the fact that they, and others doing similar work, are answering the various demands that assumptions of collective guilt have thrust upon American Muslims. It's fair to ask why more people don't know about what they are doing.

They just keep plugging away without much fanfare. I'm not sure they have much choice.

On March 3, 2017, just a little over a year after Mona Haydar, Moina Shaiq, and Robert Azzi began making themselves publicly available, Dr. Saeed Al-Bezreh appeared at an Ask a Muslim event at the public library in Centerville, Ohio. According to a report in the *Dayton Daily News*, Dr. Al-Bezreh described what it's been like being Muslim in the decades after September 11: "We realized that as professionals, as parents, as students, that we had a new title now that sits next to our professional title or whatever we are doing, and that's a Muslim. We were put under the spotlight where we had to explain ourselves to the rest of America. We were not trained for that. We were not given any warning, but we had to do it."

That's the demand we've been talking about. The attacks of September 11 are part of the history of that demand, but more recent developments have created a sense of urgency that American Muslims have not been able to ignore. For Yousuf Raheem, who helped organize a mosque open house in Waltham, Massachusetts, in May 2016, the contemporary conditions of public life require a response. "It's an extra burden we have to prove of ourselves and we take the challenge and do it as much as we can," he told the *Waltham News Tribune*.

This burden extends even to American Muslims who have lived and worked in the same local communities for decades.

The origins of Islamic Center of Fredericksburg, which we discussed earlier, date back to 1986 when Muslim families new to the area began to organize. After the events at the planning meeting in late 2015, which took many members by surprise, the mosque began hosting interfaith potlucks.

"That was the shocking thing," Samer Shalaby, whom you previously met, told the *New York Times*. "People don't realize that they have a mosque next door." Despite having been an unassuming part of the community for many years, the larger conditions of public life demanded that the members of the mosque prove themselves to their neighbors. "Letting people in the mosque opens it up," Samer added. "It shows it's not suspicious."

Members of the Islamic Center of Fredericksburg needed to open up their space in an effort to ensure that they could be in public spaces, such as town planning meetings, without fear of being confronted by anti-Muslim vitriol. They felt that they needed to humanize themselves in order to engage in public life in the community where they live—even though some of them have been living and working there for generations.

Such is the power of the paths that anti-Muslim activists have prepared for people to follow in recent years. For some non-Muslim Americans, like those confronting Samer, the appeal of these paths is stronger than the personal, accumulated experience of community life lived alongside Muslims.

In some cities and towns, where Muslims might not have been residents for as long as Samer Shalaby's family has been living in Fredericksburg, there might be less personal experience of shared community life to draw on. This creates a pressing need to make new connections. Salih Erschen, who co-founded the first mosque in Janesville, Wisconsin, five years ago, has taken a proactive approach to providing area residents with an alternate, nonsuspicious path to take.

When they first arrived in town, Salih and his wife, Yasmin, distributed leaflets about their mosque and knocked on doors introducing themselves. Two years later, they were continuing to encourage people to visit the mosque. "We make ourselves open to communicate with people if they have questions," Salih told the *Janesville Gazette* in 2017.

"Generally, people know nothing about Islam at all. A big topic is related to violence and terror in the world. I call them psychological landmines. They are important to address because people have a lot of anxiety about them."

For Salih and other members of the Janesville mosque, an open-door policy—including for all prayer services, and more specific invitations, such as their 2017 "Fast with a Muslim" initiative during Ramadan—is essential to creating an alternative to the path that anti-Muslim rhetoric prepares. One mosque member, Assad Mirza, said, "What I have found throughout my life in the United States is that people are interested in who I am as a practitioner of Islam. The mosque lets us connect as humans and talk about other things later."

Ramadan, a monthlong celebration that recognizes the first revelations of the Qur'an, is an especially popular time of year for mosques to host gatherings. Many organizers of such outreach events, which often involve meals to break the daylong fast that for many Muslims is an important practice during Ramadan, talk about the value of eating together to create human connections.

In May 2017 in Morton Grove, Illinois, for example, members of the Muslim Education Center hosted nearly three hundred people for an interfaith iftar dinner to celebrate Ramadan. According to a report in the *Daily Herald*, as all the participants shared a meal, Christian, Jewish, Muslim, Baha'i, and Hindu religious leaders demonstrated human connections across different traditions by talking about the place of food and fasting in their communities.

Not all outreach events that involve the humanizing power of food are quite at that scale. Growing anti-Muslim sentiment in 2015 and 2016, and especially the rhetoric of the 2016 election, left a Seattle resident named Amanda Saab feeling— much like Moina Shaiq—that she had to do something out of the box to address the situation. Her idea? "Dinner with Your Muslim Neighbor."

Amanda is an accomplished chef and thought that intimate gatherings over good food would provide the perfect environment to connect with people on a human level. With a wide social media following thanks to her successful 2015 run on *MasterChef*, Dinner with Your Muslim Neighbor quickly became a regular event. She and her husband, Hussein, invited strangers into their home for a free meals and conversation, and eventually began putting out calls for other people to host similar events, for which Amanda prepared food as well.

They continued to host Dinner with Your Muslim Neighbor events after they moved to Michigan to be closer to family. They even purchased and prepared a dinner for an event in April 2017 when they returned to Seattle on vacation. Jewish acquaintances offered to host the event, which coincided with Passover. Amanda made sure that everything was kosher, and the meal was punctuated by Arabic and Hebrew blessings. As they always do when they host others, many of whom have been complete strangers, Amanda and Hussein answered any questions that dinner guests had.

Since starting her venture, Amanda has worked with an acquaintance to create toolkits for others who want to hold Dinner with Your Muslim Neighbor events. What is striking about Amanda's story is the way that she talked about the thought process that led her to turn to Hussein one day and say, "Let's invite strangers over for dinner."

In an interview with the *Washington Post* in May 2017, Amanda described the way she began feeling as anti-Muslim sentiment grew around her, both in her own direct experience as well as what she was seeing at the national level. She was hit with the realization that many people must not know Muslims. That's the only reason she could think of for the way that so many people were talking about and treating Muslims.

"Have I played a part in that?" she asked. "Have I not reached out to people and given them an opportunity to meet me?" Much like Moina Shaiq, she wanted to make sure that, even as just one person, she was doing all she could to make sure that non-Muslims had the chance to meet someone who's Muslim.

As Amanda and Hussein began building their own careers and thinking about starting a family, they knew they had to scale back the number of events they hosted. That's when she started working on the toolkit, so that maybe her initiative would inspire others.

The everyday American Muslims like those we've met here, who are working so hard to humanize Muslim public life, in fact do appear to be inspiring others. In February 2018, for example, Muqaddas Ejaz, Evana Cooper-Starling, and Nertila Cana worked together to plan the "Know Your Muslim Neighbor" campaign in Cherry Hill, New Jersey, which kicked off with an event at a public library. In an interview with the *Philadelphia Inquirer*, they make it clear that they have been inspired by what other American Muslims have been doing. The article mentions Moina Shaiq and Amanda Saab as particularly significant examples of such work.

We Are Just Average, Boring Folk

In 2018, Muslim communities across the country continued to host mosque open houses, participate in interfaith initiatives, gather people around meals, stand in public with signs urging people to say hello and ask questions, and otherwise make themselves available to non-Muslims. They have been answering the demands of others to an extent that far exceeds what anyone could reasonably expect of a community that totals less than 1 percent of the country's population.

Speaking with the *East Bay Times* in 2018, Munir Safi, who helps coordinate public outreach efforts for five mosques in Hayward, California, explained in clear terms why he thinks it's vital for Muslims to be tireless in these efforts.

He said, "I'm an American who just so happens to be Muslim in the sense that I'm just living, have a family and my own aspirations. In the middle of all this, I want to make sure our community is represented because I feel that if we don't tell our stories, somebody will readily tell that story and it might not be with the right bent. It might be someone who is Islamophobic and will happily tell our story." Throughout this book, we have seen what can happen when that's the case.

The way he describes them, his goals are pretty modest. "I think it's just a matter of normalizing ourselves in the community and saying that we're really just average folk and pretty boring, actually. That's the message I'm trying to put across—it really is—and it's sad that we have to do this, to say that we are boring, average folk."

Even modest goals, though, can be much harder to reach than they seem like they should be. Way back in 2009, before what I've described as the rehabilitation of public hate even began, a teenager in Baton Rouge put it so well. Speaking to the *Advocate* back in 2009, Noor Alshibli had this to say about being Muslim in America: "The toughest thing is getting people to understand you and that you are human." This challenge has deepened since then.

For much of the past decade, American Muslims across the country have been striving diligently to accomplish this goal. They have tried to create a path for public life—for Muslims and non-Muslims alike—that provides alternatives to what anti-Muslim activists offer. By one measure, at least, we may be seeing the results of all that hard work.

The Muslims Are Coming!

In what remains a high-water mark, at least seven hundred American Muslims ran for elected office in 2000 at all levels of government. In 2002, that number had decreased by about 90 percent to seventy.[4] Data suggests that the numbers did not increase significantly in the years 2002–2010. In fact, they appear to have actually decreased more over time.

In 2009 and 2010, a total of ten American Muslim candidates running for elected office received media attention. All of the races were for local or statewide posts. I want to emphasize that this is not an exhaustive tally. It reflects only those candidates whose races attracted coverage in mainstream media sources. But at the very least it suggests that by one important measure, American Muslim participation in public life at the end of decade looked considerably different than before September 11, 2001.

There were some notable electoral successes for American Muslims between 2001 and 2010. Keith Ellison, representing a Minneapolis-area district, entered Congress in 2005, while André Carson, representing an Indianapolis-area district, entered in 2008 via special election. A number of American Muslims were also appointed to important political positions in Washington, among them Arif Ali Khan and Kareem Shohra at the Department of Homeland Security, both in 2009.

These developments are without question significant milestones in the history of American Muslim communities. When set side by side with data about decreases in Muslims standing for office as well as about American Muslim participation in public life more generally, though, we can see that these amazing developments are part of a more complex picture.

In contrast to the ten American Muslim individuals whose candidacies received media attention in 2009 and 2010, my students and I found media coverage of around three hundred instances of Muslim communities engaging in "humanizing work" during the same period. The ratio between these two figures remained similar for much of the 2010s.

While running for office and humanizing work are by no means the only ways of measuring engagement in public life, these numbers do provide further insight into the scale of efforts to simply humanize Muslim public life. We can't ever know how many other American Muslims would have stood for office if not for the demand for particular kinds of public engagement.

Then, in the 2017–2018 election cycle, something began to change. Just as 2017 marked the highpoint of American Muslim humanizing work in the period from 2010 to 2018, more American Muslims decided to run for elected office in the 2017–2018 cycle than had since 2000. By some estimates, at least one hundred American Muslims ran for local, state, and federal elections. My students and I found media coverage of about seventy-five.

In 2016, Ilhan Omar became the first Somali American legislator elected in the United States. Just two years later, in 2018, after having spent nearly a decade working her way up through the ranks of local and state politics, she became one of the first two American Muslim women to join Congress. Speaking to Wajahat Ali, an author, playwright, and lawyer, for an article in the *New York Times* about American Muslims running for office called "The Muslims Are Coming!" Omar explained her motivations.

"It is important that people recognize I am someone who is a public servant working to create a better society, who just happens to be a Muslim refugee."

This is a sentiment that candidates across the country echo. Speaking to the *Minnesota Post*, Harris Pasha, who ran for a seat in the Minnesota state House in 2018, said, "It's not enough to be just a Muslim. I think we really need someone who's going to do the work of unearthing the mechanisms of law and policy and how that actually interacts with people's lives." Like Omar, he wants to be a good public servant who happens to be Muslim.

Hadiya Afzaal, who ran for a seat on the Dupage County board in Illinois in 2018, wanted to help streamline county government, raise the county tobacco purchase age to twenty-one, and bring an ethic of environmental conversation to county government. While in the picture accompanying her *Daily Herald* candidate profile she is wearing a headscarf, she makes no mention of being Muslim. She ran on issues, not identity.

Her goals were the same as those of many of the American Muslims doing humanizing outreach work in recent years. As Ahmedulhadi Sharif, the imam at the Islamic Center of Tennessee, told the *Nashville Tennessean* about the open house he and his congregation hosted in October 2018, "We just want people to get to know us—that we are regular people—to build relationships, to collaborate, to make Nashville a better place, to work on common causes." People just want to make their communities better places—for everyone.

Still, for many American Muslims running for office, anti-Muslim sentiment is a constant reminder that things aren't quite that simple.

When Fardousa Jama decided to run for city council in Mankato, Minnesota, in 2018, she did what any good candidate would do. She went door to door to meet people and learn about what was important to them. Jama reported to the *Minnesota Post* that some people told her to go back from where she came from, while others let her know that they didn't support terrorists. One gentleman spat on her and told her to get off his property.

For Azra Baig, whom we met in chapter 3 and who ran for reelection to the school board in South Brunswick, New Jersey, in January 2017, anti-Muslim hostility served as a motivator to work even harder. When people vandalized her campaign signs, writing things like "ISIS Sympathizer" and "Raghead," she decided that her candidacy was more important than her discomfort.

"It made me more determined to win because I wanted to prove to these people, to whoever was doing this, I'm going to win the election and I'm going to win against hate and racism," she told *USA Today*.

Comments like this one illuminate the fact that, despite just wanting to be public servants, American Muslims who run for office are still doing humanizing work. They need to prove that they don't have a "Muslim agenda," that like many other people who are seeking to serve the public they just want to make their communities better places for everyone. American Muslims who take the courageous plunge to run for elected office simply aren't able to do so on their own terms.

There are always constraints when we put ourselves forward for things. Circumstances will always shape the decisions we make, and this includes the demands that other people make of us. Yet for many people in the United States who choose to run for elected office, this doesn't include the demand to prove that they are human.

Still, the fact that so many American Muslims ran for elected office in 2017 and 2018—and the fact that a good number were elected—signals that perhaps something is changing. Before we get ahead of ourselves, though, and risk falling into a false sense of security about the inevitable progress of American society, it's important to note that people who openly voice anti-Muslim sentiments were also elected across the country, including to Congress. Both of these things are true at the same time.

The election of more Muslims is good news because it suggests at least some broad public comfort with American Muslims in public life, but it doesn't necessarily cancel out the fear that comes from other elected officials saying anti-Muslim things and promoting anti-Muslim policies. Addressing this fear will require non-Muslim allies who are willing to follow the path for public life that American Muslims have been carefully tending. There are certainly already non-Muslim allies who are reaching out to Muslim communities with invitations to interfaith events and who are dropping by mosque open houses and attending other outreach and engagement events that we've been discussing. But not everything needs to be about events. Allyship often plays out in little ways that require more and more non-Muslims to decide, like Azra Baig, that working for the common good is more important than their own potential discomfort.

Saying Hello: A Model for Public Life

The two paths of public life we've discussed in this book—one trodden by anti-Muslim activists and another by American Muslims and their allies—are still very much open. American Muslims have shown remarkable courage in responding to other people's demands by welcoming people into their places of worship, even after they've been vandalized, and inviting strangers to coffee or into their homes for meals. This has helped clear a path that will hopefully lead to greater and greater opportunities for American Muslims to participate in public life on their own terms—a privilege that I, like perhaps many of you, have enjoyed my whole life.

The Muslims are in fact coming—they are seeking to become more a part of American public life than ever in the post–September 11 era. For those in American Muslim communities, I hope that this book has made it clear that there are non-Muslims out there who are thinking of you and the challenges you face. I hope it has helped to demonstrate—if it wasn't already—that there are lots of other Muslims in the United States working to make their communities better for everyone. You are not alone.

* * *

There are many little things that we can do to overcome fear and fear mongering and create the circumstances for all American citizens to engage in public life freely and on their own terms. They aren't grand. They don't need to be. Being a good ally is often about the little things.

For those non-Muslims who have stuck with this book, I hope you will join me in actively welcoming the incredible efforts of American Muslims to engage in public life, as many people across the country have done and are doing. But there need to be more of us.

If you read about a mosque open house in your area, stop in for a moment.

If you read about an Ask a Muslim event or a Meet a Muslim event, go.

If you are a person with religious commitments and you hear about an interfaith event, check it out.

If there is someone who is Muslim running for elected office in your town, and you agree with their policy ideas, volunteer for them.

Back in late 2015, when the conditions of public life were becoming more and more toxic for American Muslims, Iman Jodeh, who helped organize an interfaith event in Denver, Colorado, told the assembled audience (as reported by the *Denver Post*), "You all have a willingness to stand against the status quo. Thanks for extending hands and simply saying 'Hello.'" Sometimes a simple "Hello" goes really far in helping others feel like public space belongs to them, too.

We can think of saying hello in literal terms. A lot of the time that's what situations call for. But we can also think about it in a larger sense. In appropriate circumstances, "Hello" opens the possibility of further conversation. It doesn't need to be long. It just needs to communicate that you see them as a person.

One way to do this is to show that you understand that they have a life that goes beyond your interaction with them. Ask basic questions that aren't about their being Muslim. These are the kinds of conversations that your Muslim neighbors also want to have. Think about this when you see or hear about open mosque events or a Meet a Muslim event or when Muslims at the college or university in your area hold open events about Islam or Muslim cultures.

Supporting American Muslim outreach work—and saying "Hello"—is one way to travel down and further cultivate a path that creates welcoming conditions of public life. This is one way we can be good allies to Muslims in the United States. Sometimes, though, it's also important to look within our own communities, our own families, and perhaps ourselves to see how we can be good, or better, allies.

If you're at a family function and someone says something about Muslims that you feel is an overgeneralization, ask them to clarify what they mean.

If you're at a family function and someone says something outright hostile about Muslims, ask what makes them feel that way.

The same goes for hanging out with friends or colleagues. Don't shame people. Keep asking good, careful questions that gently push them to think critically about what they might have heard elsewhere.

If you're talking to someone who says that Muslims don't speak out against extremism and terrorism, introduce them to some of the people you've met in this book. And tell them that there are many other people doing similar work across the country. If you know them well enough, maybe you can even help them find out when there is a mosque open house or similar kind of event in the area.

If a new Muslim-owned business opens in your town or neighborhood, stop in and let them know you're happy that they're there.

If someone is running for election in your town, city, or state and you generally like their policies but they have said objectionable things about Muslims, then consider that as something that disqualifies them for elected office. Chances are there is an alternative who supports similar policies without the hate. They need to represent everyone, after all.

If you hear of an event about Muslims or Islam that seems to be designed to provoke or to spread fear, choose not to participate—or if you do go, ask honest questions that will make it hard for the speaker or speakers to speak in general terms that don't reflect the reality of the vast, vast majority of Muslim lives.

At the same time, being a good ally does not require being an apologist. Not all Muslims are good people or even nice people. Some Muslims have done, and will do, some pretty awful things. Generalizing about groups of people in good ways can be bad, too, because *all* generalizations just aren't true. Papering over real problems doesn't really improve anything. It doesn't make people's fears go away.

Being a good ally in some of the small ways I suggest above may very well create the conditions of public life that will put Muslims themselves in the best position to address those fears. The less afraid that people are about what other people might say or do to them, the less they'll feel like they have to constantly minister to other people's fears. This might actually mean that they are in more of a position to have debates within their own communities about issues that concern us all, like extremism.

Being a good ally to Muslims—and to other people in vulnerable communities—in some of the ways outlined here might very well be a good way to counter extremism in every community, including those to which we belong. These efforts will help to humanize not just Muslim public life, but our public lives in general.

American Muslims serve as an example to others because so many of their relatively small number in the United States have done, and continue to do, such an amazing job meeting fear head on with openness and transparency. Yet this is a burden that no vulnerable community ought to bear. The burden to humanize oneself and others with whom we might share elements of our identities because of other people's fears cuts against a core principle of our democracy: that all of us have the right to decide when, where, how, and why to participate in public life.

The above list of practical steps non-Muslims can take to be good allies to Muslims is a mix of reaching out, of making an effort to say hello, and encouraging others within our own circles to follow a path of public life that welcomes everyone in equal measure. But we can generalize these same steps to thinking about creating a welcoming public life for all vulnerable communities of people.

Fear occupies far too much space in our lives. We don't all have the same fears. Our fears, though, especially when they aren't connected to immediate threats in our lives, have the same effect. They lead us to lose our capacity to see others as human, as people who themselves struggle, who themselves have fears, who themselves feel vulnerable. Many times in our country's history, fear has led otherwise honorable people to advocate, or at least be ambivalent about, horrible treatment of vulnerable communities. Our moment is no different.

Taking small, concrete steps in our lives to create a more welcoming public life for all does not mean ignoring threats to our own safety and well-being or that of those we love. It means maintaining a habit of asking where are fears come from, how connected they are to the realities of our lives, and how we can address those fears without compromising what the vast majority of Americans think is *the* characteristic that makes us American: a deep belief in treating people equally. This is our touchstone.

Conclusion

In July 2018, not even two years after she described being Muslim in America as living with fear in your heart, Maheen Haq wrote an open letter to her hometown's mayor, Robert Bruchey II. The letter, which appeared in the *Baltimore Sun*, called out the mayor for posting anti-Muslim messages on Facebook.

The letter begins:

> Recently, you wrote on your Facebook page that you didn't blame Donald Trump for cancelling his January trip to London, and you posted a picture of London's mayor, the first Muslim elected to the post, followed by this comment: "Who would want to visit with this terrorist leading London?"
>
> So, you inherently associate Muslims with terrorists. Not knowing who we are you lump us into the category of murderers.

She then goes on to cover some of the same ground she did in 2016. She describes what it was like growing up in Hagerstown, Maryland, as a Muslim girl and young woman. "Let my experiences help you understand."

In her 2016 op-ed, Maheen promised that she'd no longer hold her tongue. She promised that she'd speak her mind. She promised that she'd defend her country's foundational values, and draw on Islam to do so.

Her 2018 letter grows out of those promises.

> Mr. Mayor, I ask you. Am I not human? Am I not guaranteed the same right to equality because of a cloth that sits upon my head?
>
> Mr. Mayor, little girls come up to me at the mosque and they ask me what to say when someone yells at them for their religion, when some-

one calls them a murderer. Mr. Mayor, why am I teaching the daughters of my community how to fight bigotry when they should be learning how to read?

Mr. Mayor, my parents and my religion have taught me:

You fight anger with love, hate with kindness, and violence with peace.

But I was also taught that righteousness is not to swallow oppression; righteousness is to fight for justice and equality.

Maheen and her community invited the mayor to visit her mosque, which he did.

Only time will tell if the visit changes the mayor's perceptions of Muslims, as Maheen was hoping. Either way, Maheen was making good on *her* promise. She was kind enough to talk with me about what made it possible to work through the fear in her heart to openly criticize someone in a position of power in her own hometown.[1]

The letter is a reflection of a larger process of growth and change. After she wrote her 2016 op-ed, Maheen traveled to Jordan to learn more about the refugee crisis gripping the Middle East for herself. She became even more active in the Muslim Student Association on her college campus. She pushed people in her own community in Hagerstown, especially those in older generations, to think broadly about equality and social justice in the United States. She inspired her mother to be a more active advocate of progressive causes.

When we spoke, I asked Maheen what she thinks of the contemporary conditions of public life, especially since she wrote her op-ed.

She answered without hesitation. "I personally feel it's gotten worse. Hate crimes have become more normalized, especially after Christchurch," she said, referencing the May 2019 attacks in which a self-professed white supremacist killed fifty-one people and injured almost fifty more in two Christchurch, New Zealand, mosques. "There was recently a fire in New Haven," an incidence of arson that destroyed a

Connecticut mosque under construction, also in May 2019. "This stuff is always happening. I'm not surprised anymore."

She said what is surprising is that hate has become so public, and not just about Muslims. "Anti-Semitism has become very bold, too." This is why, like many Muslims around the country, she sees being a good ally as essential to her life.

If things have gotten worse, I asked her, what has made it possible to work through the fear in her heart that she described in her 2016 op-ed to voice her opinions more publicly?

The conditions of public life have changed her, she told me. It has deepened her faith.

She told me a story about an experience she had, when she was driving alone and a man was yelling at her as she tried to turn her car around in a dead-end. She described sitting in a parking lot crying afterward. She imagined herself dying. She came to terms with the fact that something could happen to her at any time, that she was not ultimately in control of her destiny.

She decided that this was the ultimate motivation to live without regret. To live a life that she could be proud of.

"I don't feel afraid anymore. I don't feel scared. This is my reality." Later in the conversation, she asked, "What can you do to someone who's not afraid?"

Maheen's commitment to being an advocate for others, in part by being a vocal critic of injustice, is inspiring. "It's incumbent. It's necessary. You have to. There's no question."

She wants to create a better world for others, including her own small cousins. "I don't want them to grow up being afraid," she said. "It's not a way to live."

* * *

As I listened to Maheen speak, I thought about how religious studies scholar Sylvia Chan-Malik talks about living as a member of a vulnerable community in her book *Being Muslim: A Cultural History of Women of Color in American Islam*. She describes a feeling of "againstness," of living in such a way that you're always bumping up against hostile social norms and practices simply because of who you are. It's a life of constantly being on guard.

This is not the life I want for my friends. It's not the life that I want for anyone. Maheen's resiliency in the face of fear is beautiful and inspiring. And yet. It's heartbreaking.

Fear is a normal part of being human, but what we do with our fear is not preordained. It's a choice. It's a series of choices, every day. Let's make the right ones together by being good allies to one another, even when it's hard.

Especially when it's hard.

ACKNOWLEDGMENTS

My name may be on this book, but scholarship never happens without the support and collaboration of others. Reaching back many years, Nancy and Paul supported my desire to become a scholar with the hope that I would do work that draws people together. It's *my* hope that *Fear in Our Hearts* does that in some small way.

I am immensely grateful to work at Grinnell College, an institution that in many different ways supports scholarship whose immediate and explicit goal is to make the world a better place. My colleagues in religious studies and history have been supportive and encouraging as my work has moved in that direction. Rachel Schnepper opened up a whole new world to me, in part by introducing me to Roopika Risam, but also just by being her indefatigable self and helping me dream big. Erik Simpson was a tireless advocate for the research behind this book, connecting me to the generous funding from the Mellon Foundation that made a project called Mapping Islamophobia, from which this book derives, possible.

Over the past five years, I've had the opportunity to collaborate with some truly outstanding students at Grinnell. They played an instrumental role in the foundational research for this book. I'd like to especially acknowledge Julia Schafer and Farah Omer for their exceptional commitment to Mapping Islamophobia.

Moving from Mapping Islamophobia to *Fear in Our Hearts* was made possible by Kecia Ali, whose kind and generous mentorship has touched many people. I feel lucky to be among them. I'm also fortunate to have benefited from the guidance of Carey Newman, whose masterful critiques and guidance never left me in doubt about what this book could be or my ability to bring it to life.

Writing a book, from articulating kernels of ideas to the nuts and bolts of daily work, requires endless support from friends and colleagues. Shannon Dunn opened an opportunity to present an early version of the book's argument at Gonzaga University and was a patient and kind reader as the project progressed. My sabbatical buddy, Karla Erickson, is an incredible inspiration. Her feedback, along with that of my other writing retreaters, Carolyn Lewis and Albert Lacson, always came at just the right time and in just the right spirit. Aysha Hidayatullah has been a dear friend and intellectual companion since we met many years ago. Our weekly check-ins throughout the writing process were a true blessing.

Many more friends and colleagues supported this project at various stages. The good folks at the Wabash Center for Teaching and Learning Theology and Religion offered seed funding early on. Faculty, staff, and students at Eckerd College, Lehigh University, and Northwestern University offered opportunities to share parts of the project along the way and to expand my professional community.

Jennifer Hammer and NYU Press have been a dream to work with. Professional. Efficient. Supportive. Jennifer has gently pushed me to pull out the biggest story I could tell. I couldn't have asked for a better landing spot for this project.

There would be no project, of course, without all of the amazing work that Muslims across the country are doing to make our world a better place. They have looked and continue to look fear in the eye and choose to open themselves to the world around them. May we all take note. Maheen Haq, who embodies this spirit, has given her time and support to this project. Thank you, Maheen.

Finally, I'd like to acknowledge the people who are closer to me than my own veins—Tina and Kiran. Tina's fierce intellect challenges me and pushes me to learn more and to expand my horizons, to grow more than I ever could have imagined. Kiran's compassionate commitment to making the world a more welcoming place for everyone is a constant inspiration. I'm a lucky Papa. I hope this book makes her proud.

FOR FURTHER READING

You've encountered an array of amazing sources in the notes that explore key themes in the book. Below, you'll find a carefully selected list of sources for further reading. Many of them are books, but there are some articles and chapters of books as well. Most, but not all, appear in the notes. Some are more "scholarly," while others are written for a broader audience. Please consider them as good places to begin digging a little deeper into a topic or topics that may be of particular interest to you. There is a lot of thematic overlap across the sources in each category, but hopefully they can help you organize your search.

ISLAMOPHOBIA AND ANTI-MUSLIM HOSTILITY

Carl Ernst, ed., *Islamophobia in America: The Anatomy of Intolerance* (New York: Palgrave Macmillan, 2013). The essays in this volume cover a number of topics, including Islamophobia in different cultural settings, histories of Islamophobia in the United States, and the role that gender plays in anti-Muslim hostility. Authors include Kambiz GhaneaBassiri, Edward Curtis, Peter Gotschalk and Gabriel Greenberg, Andrew Shyrock, and Juliane Hammer.

Todd Green, *The Fear of Islam: An Introduction to Islamophobia in the West* (Minneapolis: Fortress Press, 2015; 2nd ed., 2019). Green's book provides an excellent history and overview of Islamophobia in Europe and the United States.

Todd Green, *Presumed Guilty: Why We Shouldn't Ask Muslims to Condemn Terrorism* (Minneapolis: Fortress Press, 2018). Green's follow-up to *The Fear of Islam* provides a look at how a common practice—asking Muslims to condemn terrorism and extremism—creates dangerous double standards regarding the relationship between religion(s) and violence and ignores the work that Muslims are already doing around the world to combat extremism.

Juliane Hammer, "Muslim Women, Anti-Muslim Hostility, and the State in the Age of Terror," in *Muslims and US Politics Today*, ed. Mohammad Khalil (Cambridge, MA: Harvard University Press, 2019), 104–123. Hammer explains why gender is an essential consideration in understanding how anti-Muslim hostility functions. Other essays in this volume will be of note as well depending on your particular interests.

ISLAM AND MUSLIMS IN THE UNITED STATES

Ala Alryyes, trans. and ed., *A Muslim American Slave: The Life of Omar ibn Said* (Madison: University of Wisconsin Press, 2011). The book includes the only known autobiography written by an enslaved Muslim in the United States and presents a collection of essays from scholars that provide information about him and the larger historical and cultural context of his life. Contributors include Sylviane Diouf, Michael Gomez, and Allan Austin.

Edward Curtis, *Muslims in America: A Short History* (New York: Oxford University Press, 2009). Curtis provides a very accessible overview of the long and complex history of Muslims in the United States and the Americas.

Carl Ernst, *Following Muhammad: Rethinking Islam in the Contemporary World* (Chapel Hill: UNC Press, 2003). Ernst isn't focusing on Islam and Muslims in the United States per se, but the book offers a remarkably accessible introduction to the study of Islam. This includes what it means to study Islam in a post–September 11 world.

Zareena Grewal, *Islam Is a Foreign Country: American Muslims and the Global Crisis of Authority* (New York: NYU Press, 2014). Grewal places Islam and Muslims in the United States within broader contexts of Muslim communities worldwide, raising important questions about what counts as "the Muslim world" and why. The book's introduction offers an accessible discussion of some very complex questions.

Amir Hussain, *Muslims and the Making of America* (Waco, TX: Baylor University Press, 2016). Hussain offers a look at the long history of Muslims in the United States through the contributions that particular individuals have made.

Denise Spellberg, *Thomas Jefferson's Qur'an: Islam and the Founders* (New York: Vintage, 2014). Spellberg offers an important look at debates about Muslims that were part of the founding moments of the country.

RACE AND RACIALIZATION IN THE UNITED STATES

Su'ad Abdul Khabeer, "Citizens and Suspects: Race, Gender, and the Making of American Muslim Citizenship," *Transforming Anthropology* 25, no. 2 (2017), 103–119. Abdul Khabeer explores the roles that race and gender play in how individuals experience anti-Muslim hostility in the United States and how this relates to peoples' ability to experience belonging and enjoy the full rights of citizenship.

Mathew Frye Jacobson, *Whiteness of a Different Color: European Immigrants and the Alchemy of Race* (Cambridge, MA: Harvard University Press, 1998). Jacobson tells a fascinating story of how the category of "whiteness" has changed over time in the United States along with patterns of immigration.

Nell Irvin Painter, *The History of White People* (New York: W.W. Norton, 2010). Painter provides an accessible history of "whiteness" that weaves together a remarkable number of threads, including whiteness across history and, focusing more on the United States, race and science, race and politics, enslavement, and immigration.

Saher Selod, *Forever Suspect: Racialized Surveillance of Muslim Americans in the War on Terror* (New Brunswick, NJ: Rutgers University Press, 2018). Selod offers an overview of how "Muslim" became a defining racial identity in the United States in the context of the War on Terror and how this affects the citizenship status of America Muslims.

Moustafa Bayoumi, *How Does It Feel to Be a Problem? Being Young and Arab in America* (New York: Penguin Press, 2008). Bayoumi offers various answers to the question in the book's title in the form of experiences of seven different people living in and around New York City in the wake of September 11, 2001. These stories beautifully capture the nuance and complexity of belonging.

Angela Onwuachi-Willig, "The Trauma of the Routine: Lessons on Cultural Trauma from the Emmett Till Verdict," *Sociological Theory* 34, no. 4 (2016), 335–357. Onwuachi-Willig explores how the threat and reality of routine harm to individuals from vulnerable communities affects their sense of belonging in broader social and political contexts—and what conditions need to be in place for these experiences to give rise to social change.

Rachel Pain and Susan Smith, "Fear: Critical Geopolitics and Everyday Life," in *Fear: Critical Geopolitics and Everyday Life*, ed. Rachel Pain and Susan Smith (London: Ashgate, 2008), 1–19. This essay explores the effect that fear, especially fear operating at a mass scale, has on people's capacity to live inclusive, welcoming public lives or, conversely (for people in vulnerable groups), to participate fully in community life.

Joe Painter and Chris Philo, "Spaces of Citizenship: An Introduction," *Political Geography* 14, no. 2 (1995), 107–120. Painter and Philo use the idea of "socio-cultural citizenship" to discuss the role of access to public space in how people experience the realities of everyday citizenship and belonging.

Nira Yuval-Davis, "Belonging and the Politics of Belonging," *Patterns of Prejudice* 40, no. 3 (2006), 197–214. Yuval-Davis provides a very useful framework for understanding how "belonging" works, especially in situations in which people enjoy more or less privilege in a given context. She argues that belonging includes emotional attachments of individuals as well as the larger social and political structures that frame our everyday lives.

PREFACE

1 The term "Islamophobia" first appeared in a 1991 report by the
Runnymede Trust, a British organization dedicated to equality in
the United Kingdom. Their report defined Islamophobia as
"unfounded hostility towards Muslims, and therefore fear or
dislike of all or most Muslims."

   Defined in this way, Islamophobia has been present in the
United States for a long time, certainly well before we began to use
the term. Even with this long history, though, there is no question
that fear or dislike of Muslims became part of public life in new
and more extreme ways after 2001. A growing number of people
began thinking that suspicion of Muslims was not unfounded.
The country had just experienced traumatic events involving
Muslims *and* more and more Muslims from around the world
were immigrating to the United States.

   It is in this context that researchers began focusing on
Islamophobia and anti-Muslim hostility and its dangerous place
in American life. This led to a number of foundational studies and
collections of essays, including *Islamophobia: Making Muslims the
Enemy*, by Peter Gottschalk (London: Rowman & Littlefield,
2007); *Islamophobia: The Challenge of Pluralism in the 21st
Century*, edited by John Esposito and Ibrahim Kalin (Oxford:
Oxford University Press, 2011); *The Islamophobia Industry: How
the Far Right Manufactures Fear of Muslims*, by Nathan Lean
(London: Pluto Books, 2012; 2nd ed., 2017); *Islamophobia in
America: The Anatomy of Intolerance*, edited by Carl Ernst (New
York: Palgrave, 2013); *Terrified: How Anti-Muslim Fringe*

Organizations Became Mainstream, by Christopher Bail (Princeton, NJ: Princeton University Press, 2015); and *The Fear of Islam: An Introduction to Islamophobia in the West*, by Todd Green (Minneapolis: Fortress Press, 2015; 2nd ed., 2019). Many other researchers have made and continue to make important contributions to this growing field. One recent contribution of note is Muhammad Khalil's *Jihad, Radicalism, and the New Atheism* (New York: Cambridge University Press, 2018), which addresses ways that Islamophobia has gained traction among critics of religion, liberal atheists among them. You'll find references to other sources in the notes that appear throughout the book.

Together, these works make a convincing case that Islamophobia has grown in influence and significance over the past couple of decades. One obvious way to chart this growth is through the analysis of Islamophobic discourses, or statements about Islam and Muslims that draw on and reinforce existing negative stereotypes. Often, these discourses portray Islam and Muslims as a fundamental threat to our country.

They draw on stereotypes that have existed in one form or another for a very long time, as Todd Green shows in *Fear of Islam*, and that have been popularized more recently by people involved with the organizations that Nathan Lean and Christopher Bail discuss. A variety of media outlets echo them and give them even further reach. These discourses contribute to the lived environment for American Muslims like Maheen Haq, a young woman you'll meet in chapter 1, who describes an environment that is full of fear.

Analyzing anti-Muslim or Islamophobic discourses and the stereotypes that drive them is a necessary step in getting a sense of the conditions of public life for American Muslims. As religious studies scholar Juliane Hammer argues, however, it is equally important to remember that the ways that people think and talk about Islam are often actually about Muslims and their bodies. Islamophobic discourses are more about Muslims and what they do—or what people think they do—than about something abstract called "Islam."

Drawing on the work of legal scholar Sahar Aziz, Hammer points out that this is particularly true for Muslim women, whose lives and bodies often figure centrally in negative stereotypes about Islam and whose attire can at times make them targets of anti-Muslim hostility. See, for example, Juliane Hammer, "(Muslim) Women's Bodies, Islamophobia, and American Politics," *Bulletin for the Study of Religion* 42, no. 1 (2013), 29–36; "Center Stage: Gendered Islamophobia and Muslim Women," in *Islamophobia in America: The Anatomy of Intolerance*, ed. Carl Ernst (New York: Palgrave Macmillan, 2013), 107–145; and "Muslim Women, Anti-Muslim Hostility, and the State in the Age of Terror," in *Muslims and US Politics Today*, ed. Mohammad Khalil (Cambridge, MA: Harvard University Press, 2019), 104–123.

Hammer's focus on embodied experiences of hostility has influenced the way I approach my work. I tend to follow Hammer in using the term "anti-Muslim hostility" more often than "Islamophobia." After all, it's Muslims who experience the effects of how people think and talk about Islam, Muslims, and what (they think) Muslims do.

Anna Mannson McGinty tries to account for the connection between how people think and talk about Islam and Muslims and how this affects Muslims themselves. She argues that there are two kinds of Islamophobia, which are related but distinct. See McGinty, "Embodied Islamophobia: Lived Experiences of Anti-Muslim Discourses and Assaults in Milwaukee, Wisconsin," *Social and Cultural Geography* (2018), 1–19, DOI: 10.1080/14649365.2018.1497192.

There is the systematic kind, which includes how people think and talk about Islam and Muslims, especially in public, and how this affects the ways that institutions, like government agencies and businesses, function. And then there is embodied Islamophobia. This refers to the more intimate manifestations and experiences of anti-Muslim hostility—face-to-face harassment, assaults, murder. Contemporary conditions of public life for American Muslims are a swirling cocktail of these two forms of anti-Muslim hostility.

The list of books above shows that there's a lot of scholarly work available on Islamophobia and anti-Muslim hostility. This includes general historical treatments; histories of particular Muslim communities in the United States; theories of how Islamophobia works; and analysis of Islamophobic media representations, government policies, the central place of gender in anti-Muslim hostility, and many other related topics. This amazing body of work includes discussion of lots of particular instances of Islamophobia and anti-Muslim hostility.

But when I began learning more about these topics, I didn't find a scholarly project that tried to capture the bigger picture of Islamophobia and anti-Muslim hostility in the contemporary United States by documenting as many individual instances as possible, combining "systematic" and "embodied" forms of the phenomena. The web-based project that I have built with my students, Mapping Islamophobia, began as an effort to do that.

2 The Mapping Islamophobia database is available for download on our website, mappingislamophobia.org. It includes information about each and every newspaper article we've read. There are lots of interactive maps about anti-Muslim activity you can explore on the website. Each dot on the maps represents an instance of anti-Muslim activity. If you click on it, you can learn more about that incident as well as the newspaper article we drew on to write about it.

3 Since we began collecting data, my students and I have docu- mented over fifteen hundred reports of anti-Muslim hostility that

occurred across the United States between 2010 and 2018. All of this data comes from media reports, most of which cite either civil rights organizations or law enforcement (or both) as sources. I draw on this data throughout this book.

My methods of collecting data on anti-Muslim hostility have their plusses and minuses, and I want to be as transparent as possible about this. The biggest minus is that by focusing on media reports I know I've missed a lot of anti-Muslim activity. The dataset on anti-Muslim hostility I've built is far from complete. This is true for a handful of reasons.

First, only a tiny fraction of what happens in the world around us ends up in the media, whether local or national. It certainly seems that local and national outlets have been focusing more attention on anti-Muslim hostility recently. This may be a reflection of a general increase in anti-Muslim hostility, which all data suggests has been the case over the past few years. But the relative scarcity of reports as we move back in time may also be a reflection of media outlets having given less time and attention to the topic.

Second, experts agree that reports of hate crimes fall well below what's actually happening. The Department of Justice estimates that targets in at least half of incidents that could count as hate crimes don't report their experiences to law enforcement. If we can take what we know about hate crime statistics and apply it to anti-Muslim incidents more generally, which seems like a reasonable step, we can be pretty certain people are having some terrible experiences that only the victims and their friends and families know about. Reporting mechanisms are improving, but some people—likely for a variety of complex reasons—choose to keep these experiences to themselves or within their family and friend groups.

Third, incidences of anti-Muslim hostility that don't rise to the level of hate crimes or actionable discrimination won't ever receive media attention. People experience anti-Muslim hostility without it becoming news. This means that we can't ever really know the full extent of the problem.

Finally, a fourth reason that I'm pretty certain my data is far from exhaustive has to do with how I collect information. I limit my data to reports from "print" news outlets that have publicly identified editorial boards, that attribute articles and research to actual people, and whose editorial policies ensure proper, verifiable sourcing of claims. This means that I typically don't draw from television news. I usually don't include reports that come from or appear only on social media or the websites of advocacy organizations. I also avoid news sources that don't fit traditional categories.

Unlike some of the other reasons that my data is incomplete, I have a lot of control over the way I collect information. In practice, by restricting my sources in this way I am intentionally limiting my data. Why would I do that?

Well, Islamophobia and anti-Muslim hostility create the conditions for this project, too. There have been a handful of reports about anti-Muslim incidents that proved untrue over the last few years. For conservative or right-wing media sources like Fox News, Daily Caller, Breitbart, and FrontPage Magazine, these unfortunate instances are part of a larger phenomenon of "hate crime hoaxes."

Caleb Parke, an associate editor at FoxNews.com, wrote an article in late 2017 entitled "Hate Crimes and Hoaxes: 10 Campus Stories Debunked in 2017." He refers to false reports of hate crimes on college campuses as a growing national phenomenon. In support of this claim, Parke presents a quote from an interview with Laird Wilcox, author of the self-published *Crying Wolf: Hate Crime Hoaxes in America*. Wilcox says, "I would say now 80 percent of the events that happen on campus are hoaxes or

pranks." (Wilcox's book has also inspired a website called www.
fakehatecrimes.org.)

A 2018 article in FrontPage Magazine addresses anti-Muslim
hate crime hoaxes more specifically. The author, Daniel
Greenfield, claims that the "torrent" of fake reports fundamentally distorts statistics about anti-Muslim activity in the United
States. He blames mainstream media outlets for lax reporting
practices, saying that they are more eager to push a certain
narrative about the rise of anti-Muslim hate after the 2016 election
than they are in accurate reporting.

From all that I can see in my years of collecting data, the
number of false reports about anti-Muslim incidents is not
sufficient to question the remarkable rise of anti-Muslim hostility
in the United States since late 2015. By highlighting real cases of
false reporting, however, Parke, Greenfield, and others who talk
about "hate crime hoaxes" create skepticism around the reliability
of anecdotal and empirical data on anti-Muslim hostility gathered
by advocacy organizations and federal agencies. Given that
Muslim advocacy organizations have expressed concerns about
the effects of made-up incidents, I realized pretty early on in this
project that I needed to anticipate this kind of criticism.

As a result, I have purposefully limited what is in my data on
anti-Muslim hostility. I know full well that I am excluding incidents. I have mixed feelings about this decision, though I think it's
more right than not.

Islamophobic and anti-Muslim discourses and activities are real
parts of American public life. They affect how non-Muslims think
about Muslims. They affect how American Muslims go about
their days. And they affect how I think about my project. I want
my data to be as airtight as possible so that it can't serve as a
source for anyone who is trying to question the reality or extent of
anti-Muslim hostility.

INTRODUCTION

1 You can learn more about the 2018 Grinnell poll at www.grinnell. edu/poll. The site includes information about the questions we asked, the methodologies we used to make sure that the poll represented the American public, and what we found about what Americans think about a range of issues, including national identity, religious discrimination, immigration, and the values that motivate our lives.

2 There is some fascinating work on the place of fear in contemporary American society. One book in particular, *Fear: Critical Geopolitics and Everyday Life*, which brings together a collection of scholars writing on the issue, has been very influential in the way I've been thinking about fear in general and about fear of Muslims and public hate in the United States more specifically. In their essay introducing the collection, Rachel Pain and Susan Smith explore the nature of risk and fear in general in today's United States. See Pain and Smith, "Fear: Critical Geopolitics and Everyday Life," in *Fear: Critical Geopolitics and Everyday Life*, ed. Rachel Pain and Susan Smith (London: Ashgate, 2008), 1–19.

Risk and fear, they argue, shape our lives today in unprecedented ways. They are trying to help us think critically about the role that fear plays in the everyday, hoping that we can reimagine this role in a couple of different ways. First, they want us to consider whether fear is always simply a response to an immediate threat, or if there is something a little bit more complicated going on in the way that fear emerges as a force in our lives. Second, in the age of the War on Terror, they want to help us rethink the connection between things happening at a global/geopolitical level and fear in everyday life. They argue that reconsidering the nature of fear in relation to geopolitical events and fear in our everyday lives makes it possible to imagine ways of being human that are less anxious.

Pain and Smith acknowledge that fear is a part of the human condition. Rather than accept what they consider to be its outsized role in our lives, though, they want to ask questions about where fear, as an emotion, comes from and how it works socially and politically—more specifically, they want to know how fear survives, how it worms its way into our general orientation in the world, and how we might resist or reformulate fear. The best way to do this, they argue, is not to think about fear in the abstract. Instead, they suggest starting with everyday life.

We can accomplish a couple of different things when we do this. Focusing on fear in everyday life makes it possible to see that fear "does not pop out of the heavens and hover into the ether before blanketing itself across huge segments of cities and societies; it has to be lived and made. Its making may only in very small ways be about the 'large acts' of terror that are played, replayed, revisited and reconstituted on an almost daily basis in the press." Smith and Pain want to see how global or national-scale insecurities and risk become part of everyday life in local settings, what people do with them, and how they manifest in the lives of those associated with the risk ("the fear of those who are feared," as the authors put it).

In Pain and Smith's view, contemporary living is marked by levels of fear that often outweigh the risks. This happens when fear becomes a social or collective experience rather than an individual response to an immediate situation. As such, it comes to serve as a general orientation to the world, a sense through which we begin to see everything and that can be very disconnected from our everyday lives.

Despite the fact that fear operates in some very important ways as a collective experience in our modern society, we continue to approach the risk behind that fear as if our fear were more individual—that is, a response to an immediately threatening situation. When we are faced with a concrete threat or risk, it is perfectly logical to try to avoid or remove that risk. When fear becomes a collective experience, serving as a general orientation, it is very difficult to assess the connection between what/who we perceive as a threat and the actual risk before us.

This then leads to public discourses, social practices, and political policies that reflect what Pain and Smith call moral panic more than a rational response to a material threat. (Moral panic is a defining feature of a moral geography of fear in their terms.)

Mass incarceration of African Americans, long perceived and represented in mainstream media as disproportionately criminal threats to American society, is one example. Another example are policies that encourage racial profiling of Arab Americans, Muslims in general, and those that others perceive to be Muslim.

The same logic applies to the rise in hate crimes against Muslims in the United States. These kinds of activities are much less about the threat that individuals pose to others—which the average perpetrator of such a heinous act would of course have no way of knowing—and more about a general sense that individual Muslims pose a threat or are a risk.

At the same time, it would be a mistake to think that hate crimes against Muslims in the midst of the War on Terror are simply about the perceived threat of terrorism. Pain and Smith point out that fear in everyday life isn't just a mapping of geopolitical-scale concerns onto everyday life. Anti-Muslim activity also reflects concerns that people have about their communities changing, about who is "really" American, about who belongs (in a general sense as well as in the particular spaces of public life).

In this sense, anti-Muslim activity is both a reflection of large-scale concerns, which generate a kind of collective experience of fear, as well as more local concerns about who belongs in certain communities or neighborhoods. When we consider that anti-Muslim activity isn't just about the threat of terrorism (as a geopolitical phenomenon), we can see that anti-Muslim activity is connected to harassment of and crimes against people in other vulnerable communities insofar as such activity also reflects aspects of identity that people in majority groups might consider threatening (relating to race, class, gender, sexuality).

By focusing on fear in everyday lives, we can also highlight the fear of those who are feared. It's in the lives and on the bodies of Muslims in the United States, for example, that social or collective fears of terrorism play out. This reflects what Pain and Smith see as the relationship between fear and living in some way on the margins of broader society.

Highlighting the fear of those who are feared also opens space to consider the way they resist being in this position, push back against the cultural, social, and political operations that place them the position of being feared in the first place. This is a crucial dimension of highlighting such fear because it helps move us past the sense that people in vulnerable communities are merely passive victims of other's fear.

Pain and Smith hope that by thinking critically about where fear comes from, how it's nurtured, how it becomes a social or collective phenomenon, and how the conditions of local life relate to larger geopolitical or national-level discourses in the generation of fear, we can begin to question why risk and threat have become such a dominant way of understanding the world—and of being human.

3 Scholars across a range of disciplines study hate, including law, psychology, and sociology. There is even a journal called *Hate Studies*, to which I've contributed. Even with all of this work, or perhaps because so many scholars are writing on the topic, there isn't a widely accepted definition of the concept. Scholars do seem to agree that hate is an emotion and that it is something that often motivates speech or behavior that seeks to denigrate

or harm others. Psychological approaches to understanding hate, which tend to posit that hate is something that develops within an individual and moves outward in expression, are very influential across disciplines. For an overview of approaches to studying hate influenced by this idea, see Edward Royzman, Clark McCauley, and Paul Rozen, "From Plato to Putnam: Four Ways to Think about Hate," in *The Psychology of Hate*, ed. Robert Sternberg (Washington, DC: American Psychological Association, 2008), 3–35.

I take a somewhat different approach in this book, drawing on the work of Sara Ahmed to think about hate as a fundamentally social phenomenon. You'll recognize her influence throughout this book, especially in my thinking about belonging, citizenship, and, more generally, my interest in trying to capture how public expressions of hate affect the conditions of public life for American Muslims.

Ahmed first wrote about hate in "The Organization of Hate," an article she published in 2001 (*Law and Critique* 12, 345–365). She later expanded her discussion in *The Cultural Politics of Emotion* (New York: Routledge, 2004), a book that places hate in a broader exploration of emotion as a central feature of our social lives. To introduce you to her work on hate, I'll draw from the earlier article, which focuses exclusively on the social life of that one emotion.

Ahmed offers an account of hate that differs from common psychological approaches to the subject. Rather than imagining hate as an emotion or emotions inside of someone that then move outward toward another person or people through speech or other actions, Ahmed argues that hate is fundamentally social. Hate depends on being in relation to others, even when that relation is imagined.

Ahmed agrees with one basic assumption underlying psychological approaches to studying hate, namely, that hate is an emotion. But Ahmed argues that emotion isn't just a feeling or disposition. "Emotions *do* things," she says. "We need to consider how they work, in concrete and particular ways." One of the things they do is serve as the connective tissue between the individual and the social. This function is why she differentiates between anger, which tends to focus on individuals (no matter how intensely), while hate tends to be felt toward groups of people.

When people target someone in a particular group (or someone they perceive to be in a particular group), it is not just about the individuals involved. Hate is very much about generating, maintaining, and negotiating boundaries between communities—it is essential to an understanding of a "we" that is felt to be under threat by the very presence and demands of others. This is one of the things that hate *does*.

In important ways, especially in cases that involve relationships beyond our most intimate connections, hate can create a sense of belonging within a certain group by positioning someone else as an outsider. (Conversely, love can be an essential element of in-group and out-group creation, too. As Ahmed points out, white nationalist extremists often defend their views by saying they are not born of hate for others, but rather from love for other people like them.)

Hate as a fundamentally social phenomenon doesn't just affect those who are doing the hate, though. It can have a range of profound effects on those experiencing hate. These effects can be physiological, psychological, social, or emotional—or a combination of all four. This, too, is something that hate *does*. It causes pain. For Ahmed, this kind of pain "unmakes" the world of the person who has been the object of hate. Hate crushes the spirit. Just as hating can create a sense of self in and through belonging to a certain group, being hated can create a sense of self with exclusion at its core.

Hate makes it impossible to think of others as equals. Public hate—expressions of hate toward individuals and groups in public, shared space—in turn makes it very difficult for vulnerable communities to feel like they belong in the very places they live.

4 You'll find information about these stories on Mapping Islamophobia as well. There are a number of interactive maps devoted to American Muslim outreach efforts.

CHAPTER 1. PUBLIC LIVES

1 Maheen Haq, "Being Muslim Is . . . ," *Baltimore Sun*, November 28, 2017, www.baltimoresun.com.

2 Given the incredible diversity of American Muslim communities, it doesn't necessarily make sense at first glance that there could be a common experience of anti-Muslim sentiment and activity. I've found that concept of "racialization" can offer some insight into how this could be the case.

The passage of the Immigration and Nationality Act of 1965 forever changed the racial landscape of the United States. Although immigrants from regions other than Europe had been arriving in the United States for decades if not centuries prior to 1965, immigration reform opened the doors to increased immigration from Africa, South Asia, Southeast Asia, and the Middle East. Racialization in this context refers to the process by which people from these parts of the world became part of the racial landscape of the United States, long dominated by a "black-white" distinction into which these communities didn't fit. An unfortunate, but all too real, aspect of this process is racism, or the marginalization of groups of people on the basis of their identities (or perceived identities). Racism can be both a motivating element and outcome of racialization.

Scholars have long recognized that there are visual elements to racialization. The way that people look, or rather the way others give meaning to how people look, generate meaning in social and political contexts. However, as Saher Selod argues in *Forever Suspect: Racialized Surveillance of Muslims in the War on Terror* (New Brunswick, NJ: Rutgers University Press, 2018), focusing too much on visual cues overlooks other important elements of the racialization process.

She came to this conclusion in part because people she interviewed for the book who are racially visible as white still experienced anti-Muslim hostility. Selod offers a revised definition of racialization based on her research: "the process by which bodies become racial in their lived realities because of biological and/or cultural traits as a result of the intersection and cooperation between ideologies, policies, laws, and social interactions that results in the denial of equal treatment in society."

Selod wants us to think about all of the different factors, not just biological traits or appearances, that contribute to people's experience of race and racism in their everyday lives. This includes stereotypes associated with a given group of people. For Muslims, some such stereotypes might include the idea that Muslims wear turbans, that only Muslim women cover their hair or dress modestly, that all Muslims have particular kinds of names, that all people who speak Arabic are Muslim (and that all Muslims speak Arabic), or that Muslims are predisposed to being angry or violent.

A huge range of factors contribute to how racialization happens, which can help explain how Muslims who don't appear at all alike visually can still experience race in similar ways or how people who aren't Muslim can still be targets of anti-Muslim hostility. The effects of racialization appear in different areas, from government policies to everyday interactions people have with each other.

Su'ad Abdul Khabeer states that to be racialized as Muslim is to be "neither black nor white but to have brown skin, 'Middle

Eastern' looks, and particular national origins. Muslim legibility is also marked by behaviors such as praying, carrying specific names, and displaying gendered markers like beards and heads-carves." See Abdul Khabeer, "Citizens and Suspects: Race, Gender, and the Making of American Muslim Citizenship," *Transforming Anthropology* 25, no. 2 (2017), 103–119, DOI: 10.1111/traa.12098.

3 Of all the kinds of situations I've been talking about in these last few paragraphs, we have the best statistics for how belonging affects hate crime reporting. The Bureau of Justice Statistics, which is part of the Department of Justice, estimates that between 2004 and 2015 more than 50 percent of those targeted by hate crimes did not report their experiences to law enforcement. About a quarter of those said that they didn't report because they didn't think that the police would take their experiences seriously enough to investigate. See Madeline Mascucci and Lynn Langton, *Hate Crime Victimization, 2004–2015*, special report prepared for the Bureau of Justice Statistics, June 2017, www.bjs.gov.

4 In "That Great Dust-Heap Called History: Recovering the Multiple Spaces of Citizenship," *Political Geography* 14, no. 2, 209–216, Sara MacKian reminds us that citizenship entails much more than what we commonly recognize as political activity. She is very interested in considering what it means in practice to be a citizen, "the actuality of being a citizen and acting out citizen-ship." By moving away from formal ideas of citizenship that focus almost exclusively on our interactions with political institutions, we can gather more of a sense of how people live as members of a community—and this, MacKian argues, is the stuff that makes communities go round.

In part, this is about considering how people understand what they are doing and not just how scholars of citizenship might relate what people are doing to political structures. "It is my argument," says MacKian, that "although every individual acts within a context shaped partly by their relationship with the state, the majority would not consciously see their activities as such. The *motivation* of the bulk of citizen activity is far from political in orientation." Granted, reducing the "political" to some kind of engagement with the state would be a problem, robbing the term from richer meanings having to do with power and power relationships. Fortunately, I don't think this is what MacKian is after.

Instead, MacKian wants us to think about citizenship as something that unfolds in spaces that aren't directly related to the state. Citizenship, she argues, is in part what happens in everyday life. People "do things as part of living out their daily lives, as a part of being a *full* member of their community." Even with this, MacKian wants to caution us against imagining that this translates into a singular mode of citizenship.

> There is . . . a great deal of invisible citizen activity being missed . . . because it is the more routine, less glamorous, less ostensive side to citizenship. There are active citizens and passive citizens, dutiful citizens and citizens doing nothing but demanding rights. There are citizens operating in the core, on the periphery and dipping their toes in at the fringe, individual citizens using their own powers in their own communities to help *themselves*, not just the big boys playing at committee meetings to aid others. These are the face-to-face roles and they deserve more attention than being passed off as "mundane."

The work that people do in their everyday lives, unconnected in explicit ways to political life, is a crucial element of being a full member of a community. This doesn't suggest that political activity isn't important, but rather that we shouldn't reduce citizenship to this sphere of activity alone.

There is something I find very compelling about MacKian's ideas. Her argument seems especially relevant at a moment when it's tempting to look at the increase in American Muslims voting in elections and running for office as evidence of "engagement" in public life (a marker of becoming American), when in fact the humanizing work that people have been doing, from outreach to just being good people, is evidence of engaged citizenship all along. It is, perhaps, a kind of citizenship that reflects the conditions of public life, but it is nonetheless powerful evidence of *full* participation in community life. I'll explore these ideas more in later chapters.

5 Pew Research Center, "US Muslims Concerned about Their Place in Society, but Continue to Believe in American Dream," July 26, 2017, www.pewforum.org.

6 Institute for Social Policy and Understanding, "American Muslim Poll: Participation, Priorities, and Facing Prejudice in the 2016 Elections," March 2016, www.ispu.org.

7 Institute for Social Policy and Understanding, "American Muslim Poll 2017: Muslims at the Crossroads," March 2017, www.ispu.org.

8 Democracy Fund, "Muslims in America: Public Perceptions in the Trump Era," June 2018, www.voterstudygroup.org.

9 The process of deciding what exactly counts as "being American"—or of being committed to being American, for that matter—is a complicated one. One concept that scholars have developed to explain this process is the "citizenship agenda," which I have found to be helpful.

Anouk de Koning, Rivke Jaffe, and Martijn Koster offer a helpful definition of this concept in an article from 2015: "We define citizenship agendas as normative framings of citizenship that prescribe what norms, values, and behavior are appropriate for those claiming membership of a political community." They continue, "These agendas are concerned with defining the meaning of membership in explicitly normative ways that go beyond conventional, legal formal citizenship status." See de Koning, Jaffe, and Koster, "Citizenship Agendas in and beyond the Nation-State: (En)countering Framings of the Good Citizen," *Citizenship Studies* 19, no. 2, 121–127.

In simpler terms, de Koning, Jaffe, and Koster are interested in who gets to create the parameters for what it means to be an American. Like Sara MacKian (1995), cited in a previous note, they argue that to understand how citizenship works in practice we need to think beyond formal elements, which we often associate with the state and that typically relate to civil and political rights and obligations. Lots of different actors contribute to definitions of citizenship and the policies and practices that follow.

Governments, or the state, are certainly significant actors in this process. They define what it means to be a citizen and, further, what it means to be a "good citizen" or a "bad citizen." De Koning, Jaffe, and Koster are interested in what roles non-state actors, such as corporations and nonprofit organizations, play in this process. They want us to think about what or who else helps set "citizenship agendas," which help determine what it means to be a good or bad citizen.

By focusing on lived experience, we can see that actors far beyond the state are active in setting citizenship agendas and making claims about a given political community. Reducing citizenship to formal definitions misses the complicated ways that being a citizen relates to other forms of belonging. This is especially the case when we begin thinking about belonging at different scales, moving from nation to region to city or town and to neighborhood. Being a citizen, or having one's citizenship challenged, plays out in different, though interrelated, ways depending on the scale.

De Koning, Jaffe, and Koster set out three different situations in which non-state actors play a role in influencing, setting, and/or enforcing citizenship agendas. The first regards outsourcing. Non-state actors, whether for-profit or not-for-profit, are increasingly provisioning services that were once the purview of the state, including social services, infrastructure, and security. This puts them in a position to ensure certain codes of behavior and values related to a particular citizenship agenda—and perhaps to define them as well.

The second situation entails non-state actors actively collaborating/colluding with state actors to create citizenship agendas in pursuit of particular interests or goals. This might include unions, corporations, religious organizations, advocacy organizations, or other politically minded pressure groups.

The third situation in which non-state actors are involved in setting citizenship agendas involves a more contentious relationship with the state. Here, non-state actors, which in this scenario could also include unions, corporations, religious organizations, advocacy organizations, or other politically minded pressure groups, challenge or oppose state-driven citizenship agendas.

In all three cases, the authors argue, it's important to remember that citizenship agendas are not simply mechanisms of social and political control. "They also provide people with important horizons of aspiration and action, with *full citizenship* remaining an aspiration that fuels struggles against exclusion and inequality." Of course, this does not necessarily detract from the potential of citizenship agendas to serve a purpose that is less about facilitating belonging. "Citizenship agendas may equally be taken up in pursuit of more conservative and exclusionary futures."

The fact that almost half the country thinks that Muslims aren't fully committed to being part of life in the United States plays out in a variety of ways relating to "citizenship agendas." In chapters 2, 3, and 4, I'll talk about how anti-Muslim sentiment makes its way into policy discussions at local, state, and national levels and the work that anti-Muslim activists and organizations engage in to raise suspicions about whether Muslims can truly belong—that is, whether Muslims can ever be good citizens.

10 Institute for Social Policy and Understanding, "American Muslim Poll 2017: Muslims at the Crossroads," March 2017, www.ispu.org.

11 Kambiz GhaneaBassiri provides a detailed discussion of Muslim immigration from South Asia and the Ottoman Empire in the late nineteenth and early twentieth centuries, an important historical moment in modern discussions of race and citizenship in the United States. See GhaneaBassiri, *A History of Islam in America* (New York: Cambridge University Press, 2010). GhaneaBassiri presents information drawn from court records that provide great insight into how people—plaintiffs and judges alike—talked about race and citizenship at the time. In general, he offers a thoughtful history of Islam and Muslims in the United States, including the historical and cultural context in which debates about what it meant to be white, especially regarding Muslims, were unfolding.

12 In *White Washed: America's Invisible Middle Eastern Minority* (New York: NYU Press, 2009), John Tehranian examines the role of court cases in determining what counted as "white" when it came to immigration status. He argues that in many precedent-setting decisions over a seventy-year period from 1878 to 1952 regarding race and immigration, judges ultimately depended on cultural assumptions about what it meant to "act white," even if they used the language of science to justify their views. Legal decisions, then, depended on what Tehranian calls the "performance of whiteness," including dress, speech, and in sometimes indirect ways religious expression.

13 The presence of Muslims long predates immigration at the turn of the twentieth century. There is a well-established body of literature exploring Muslim enslaved peoples in the colonial Americas and the independent United States. A good place to begin is *A Muslim American Slave: The Life of Omar ibn Said*, translated and edited by Ala Alryyes (Madison: University of Wisconsin Press, 2011). The book includes the only known autobiography written by an enslaved Muslim in the US. Alryyes translates Omar ibn Said's autobiography from its original Arabic and presents a collection of essays from scholars such as Sylviane Diouf, Michael Gomez, and

Allan Austin that provide information about him and the larger historical and cultural context of his life. The original autobiography is now in the Library of Congress. You can find out more about Omar ibn Said and the collection at www.loc.gov/collections/omar-ibn-said-collection/about-this-collection.

14 There is a growing body of literature exploring the connection between African American and Muslim histories in the United States. Richard Brent Turner's excellent historical account, *Islam in the African-American Experience* (Bloomington: University of Indiana Press, 2003), begins with a discussion of enslaved Muslims in the Americas and explores the process by which Islam became an American religion in African American communities. Edward Curtis offers a slightly different approach in *Islam in Black America* (Albany: SUNY Press, 2002). He looks at the more general topic of Islam and African American experiences through the lives and thought of a series of notable African American Muslims. Sally Howell explores the deep historical connections between African American and immigrant or immigrant-descendent Muslim communities using a place-based approach, centering on Detroit, Michigan. See Howell, *Old Islam in Detroit: Rediscovering the Muslim American Past* (Oxford: Oxford University Press, 2014).

In *Muslim Cool: Race, Religion, and Hip-Hop in the United States* (New York: NYU Press, 2016), Su'ad Abdul Khabeer explores the deep connections between blackness and Muslim experiences in the United States. She argues that blackness, as expressed in the production of and engagement with forms of popular culture, has become central to the experience of being Muslim in the United States, especially for younger generations, which in turn has significant implications for understandings of belonging in Muslim communities.

15 Belonging is a crucial dimension of people's ability to fully participate in public life on their own terms. Nira Yuval-Davis offers compelling theory about how belonging works. See Yuval-Davis,

"Belonging and the Politics of Belonging," *Patterns of Prejudice* 40, no. 3 (2006), 197–214: DOI: 10.1080/00313220600769331.

Yuval-Davis distinguishes between belonging and the politics of belonging as distinct areas of consideration. Belonging, she argues, is a process of emotional attachment. The politics of belonging, in contrast, consist of projects aimed at constructing belonging (or exclusion, I would suppose). Differentiating the two is important for understanding how/why dominant groups seek to include others in or exclude them from a larger collectivity.

Regarding belonging as an emotional attachment, Yuval-Davis identifies a number of variables that affect this process. They include things like age, race, ethnicity, class, and ability, which can, and frequently do, intersect. At the same time, people aren't always in a position to entirely control how they identify themselves, and this can affect the emotional attachments we develop and try to maintain. She says, "Constructions of self and identity . . . can, in certain historical contexts, be forced on people. In such cases, identities and belonging/s become important dimensions of people's social locations and positioning, and the relationships between locations and identifications can become empirically more closely intertwined."

Yuval-Davis's point about identities being forced on people, it seems to me, is very closely related to the politics of belonging, which Davis defines as being about boundary maintenance. She says, "the politics of belonging is concerned with . . . the boundaries of political community of belonging, the boundaries that separate the world population into 'us' and 'them.' The politics of belonging thus also include debates about what is involved in belonging to a particular community. Much of the contemporary debates on the politics of belonging surround the question of who 'belongs' and who does not, and what are the minimum common grounds—in terms of origin, culture and normative behavior— that are required to signify belonging."

It may be difficult to force a particular self-conception on someone, but if someone hears and experiences in a variety of ways, over and over again, that they don't belong because they aren't "X" identity (American?), then it seems to follow that they would begin to think of themselves as "other" in some fundamental sense. Yuval-Davis focuses on speeches and comments by public officials and political party platforms in her discussion of the politics of belonging. But it makes a lot of sense to expand "politics" here to cultural expression more generally, especially in our age of mass media.

The expansion of what constitutes the politics of belonging is significant both for how we think about efforts to include and welcome and efforts to exclude and repel. The latter is especially important when we consider anti-Muslim sentiment in the United States, where it's fair to say that there is a coordinated effort devoted to making the case that Muslims don't—and can't— belong as Americans.

In general, Yuval-Davis's work on belonging and the politics of belonging is relevant to thinking about contemporary anti-Muslim sentiment in the United States because she was writing amid debates in the United Kingdom about whether Muslims can ever truly belong after coordinated attacks on London's public transportation system in July 2005. In the United Kingdom, as in the United States, attacks perpetrated by Muslims led to a concerted effort to "contrive and maintain prejudice" against all Muslims, to use the words of Suzanne Hall, a scholar who writes about the politics of belonging.

Yuval-Davis closes with the words of Stuart Hall, a well-known and thoughtful scholar of race and belonging. The extended passage, taken from a conversation between Yuval-Davis and Hall at a conference in London about the political of belonging, directly relates to questions of immigration and being/becoming American. There is perhaps no more significant area to think about when it comes to the politics of belonging in the contemporary United States. Hall asks,

> What are the terms for groups of people from different cultural, religious, linguistic, historical backgrounds, who have applied to occupy the same social space, whether that is a city or a nation or a region, to live with one another without either one group [the less powerful group] having to become the imitative version of the dominant one—i.e., an assimilationism—or, on the other hand, the two groups hating one another, or projecting images of degradation? In other words, how can people live together in difference?

I'll add to Hall's question here. It's not just a matter of living together in difference—it's also a matter of who gets to decide what kind of difference is significant when it comes to belonging, and how those decisions play out in the lives of those who end up on the outside.

16 Given how significant the connection between public space, belonging, and citizenship is in this book, I'd like to spend more than just a little time in the notes sharing analyses from other scholars on this subject. I'll highlight three articles in particular that provide an excellent overview of how scholars think about these connections. These articles explain why formal definitions of citizenship can't entirely capture what it means to be a member of a community, how access to or exclusion from pubic space affects the way that people feel about community membership, and why exclusion from public space makes citizenship difficult, if not nearly impossible, in practice.

Formal definitions of citizenship focus on the "rights and obligations" that come with being a member of the American political community. While important, this understanding of citizenship, which emphasizes the political relationship between an individual and the state or between an individual and their fellow citizens, can't quite capture other elements that contribute to a sense of membership in a wider community.

In the late 1980s and 1990s, some scholars began paying more attention to the social-cultural aspects of citizenship, or the social and cultural factors that lead individuals and groups to *feel* more or less like citizens in the fullest sense. Nira Yuval-Davis's work on belonging and the politics of belonging, discussed in the preceding note, was part of this trend.

So, too, was "Spaces of Citizenship," a widely cited essay on public space, belonging, and citizenship by Joe Painter and Chris Philo. The authors point out that social-cultural relationships are an essential part of who gets defined as a "real" citizen. These relationships build out of things like shared histories, cultural reference points, ethnicity, race, language, and religion. Painter and Philo explain that this is a more diffuse way of understanding citizenship, but it's related to more formal political definitions because social-cultural dimensions have a significant effect on who is accepted as a member of the local communities in which everyday life unfolds. See Painter and Philo, "Spaces of Citizenship: An Introduction," *Political Geography* 14, no. 2 (1995), 107–120.

Unlike formal measures of citizenship, social and cultural dimensions of citizenship operate through informal rules and norms that often depend on the shared identities and histories of "local majorities." These informal rules and norms play a large role in determining who is included and who is excluded (in practice) from a given community. In the small, rural Midwestern town I live in, for example, being "churched" (or not) significantly affects to what extent someone can become "local" in practice.

Citizenship in an everyday sense, then, is not just about things like voting and paying taxes. It includes the capacity to take part in the life of a local community in the fullest sense. Painter and Philo include access to public space as an essential element of such participation, including the opportunity to enjoy public space without fear: "[I]f citizenship is to mean anything in an everyday sense it should mean the ability of individuals to occupy public spaces in a manner that does not compromise their self-identity, let alone obstruct, threaten or even harm them more materially." They continue,

> If people cannot be present in public spaces (streets, squares, parks, cinemas, churches, town halls) without feeling uncomfortable, victimized, and basically "out of place," then it must be questionable whether or not these people can be regarded as citizens at all; or, at least, whether they will regard themselves as full citizens . . . able to exist on an equal footing with other people who seem perfectly "at home" when moving about in public spaces.

Painter and Philo's work has influenced scholars in a wide range of areas, including political psychology.

In "Grounding Citizenship: Toward a Political Psychology of Public Space," Andrés Di Masso argues that public spaces are the natural arenas of citizenship and thus have a profound effect on the way that people experience and perform citizenship. According to Di Masso, public spaces serve important psychological functions in a variety of ways. They can be crucial to people's self-definitions. They can be important to the development of a sense of belonging in a particular social group because they are the spaces in which people interact with others in ways that make it possible, in theory, to work toward a common good. A sense of belonging depends on safe access and use of shared space. See Di Masso, "Grounding Citizenship: Toward a Political Psychology of Public Space" *Political Psychology* 33, no. 1 (2012), 123–143.

The two articles I've talked about thus far in this note are very theoretical. They are working out how to think about ways we can analyze or think about specific situations relating to belonging, citizenship, and public space. In "White Lines: The Intercultural

Politics of Everyday Movement in Social Spaces," Greg Noble and Scott Poynting provide us a specific case study to consider. See Noble and Poynting, "White Lines: The Intercultural Politics of Everyday Movement in Social Spaces," *Journal of Intercultural Studies* 31, no. 5 (2010), 489–505. Although not about the United States, you'll quickly see its relevance to this book.

Noble and Poynting draw on extensive interviews with young Arab and Muslim Australians regarding their experiences after September 11, 2001, to explore questions about belonging, public space, and citizenship. The authors consider how public discourses demonizing particular groups of people (or racial vilification) combine with everyday experiences of demeaning and insulting treatment, acts of incivility, and hate-fueled crime to effectively exclude members of those groups from functioning as citizens in practice.

The concept of public space makes it possible for Noble and Poynting to think in concrete terms about how people *experience* exclusion, how it makes them feel, and how this in turn affects their ability to be present in public life. Analyzing their interviews with young Arab and Muslim Australians, Noble and Poynting say, "It's not just that they experience racism in their lives, but that this takes away from them the possibility of full participation in spaces of local and national belonging." The experience of racism makes people think twice about going into spaces that are supposed to be open to everyone. But this is not simply about literal access to public space.

Being a participant in public life, being what Noble and Poynting call an effective citizen, requires a basic level of comfort in a variety of public spaces. The regularity of "everyday incivility," or worse, makes this virtually impossible. "These incidents obviously happen across a vast number of social sites—on the street, in shopping centers, on public transport, at work and school, and government and business. These sites are crucial to the constitution of public space."

The accumulation of experiences meant to make people feel out of place teaches people that they in fact don't belong in public space. If they feel like they don't belong in public space then there is no way for them engage in the stuff of public life—interacting with people and developing the kinds of relationships that make it possible to figure out how to tackle everyday problems that come up in community life.

Everyday social incivility, or other, more violent manifestations of hate, teach those on the experiencing end—or even members of a particular group who hear about what's happening to others in that group—that they aren't real citizens, or members of a local or national public. Noble and Poynting argue that the "victims of racial vilification are not primarily targeted for anything they might have done, they are targeted for being who they are, or rather, being who they are *where* they are (where they don't belong)" (emphasis added). We can read this passage at a number of levels.

In a literal sense, racial vilification creates conditions in which people are insecure in public spaces because they are getting clear signals that people like them don't belong where they are. In a related but somewhat less literal sense, being unwelcome in public space means that people aren't welcome in a public, or a community, whether locally or nationally. Their presence is—because of who they are—out of place.

Public space, then, is crucial to how we understand the way that hostility toward a particular group of people affects their ability to both *feel* like they belong and *act* like they belong. Analyzing the ways that hostility toward a particular group of people plays out in public space also highlights that other citizens, on the basis of who they are, are empowered to teach others that they're unwelcome, that they don't belong in public space or in a public more broadly.

Recently, Camilla Hawthorne has called on geographers to take race into consideration more systematically. The control of movement through space, she argues, has long played a central role in racial oppression. In the United States, this dates back to the slave trade and the displacement of Native communities through Reconstruction (following the Civil War), Jim Crow, and more contemporary forms of space-based discrimination like housing policy and aggressive policing in communities of color. In this view, experiences like Donte and Rashon had in Starbucks are merely extensions of long-standing practices that have been central to American public life for a very long time. The field of black geographies is drawing more attention to connections between race and space, connections that are also essential to understanding contemporary anti-Muslim hostility. See Hawthorne, "Black Matters Are Spatial Matters: Black Geographies for the Twenty-First Century," *Geography Compass* (2019), DOI: 10.1111/gec3.12468.

17 The control of access to and presence in public space for African Americans is a significant contributing factor in the emergence of what Angela Onwuachi-Willig calls an expectation of routine harm. The concept of routine harm is part of a larger idea of cultural or community-wide trauma, which we will explore in more depth later in the book. Onwuachi-Willig describes this theory in "The Trauma of the Routine: Lessons on Cultural Trauma from the Emmett Till Verdict," *Sociological Theory* 34, no. 4 (2016), 335–357, DOI: 10.1177/0735275116679864.

18 American mythologies around immigrant communities' belonging typically portray a gradual process of becoming. There are a variety of common metaphors to describe this process. The "melting pot" remains popular, but it isn't the only metaphor to describe the process of becoming American for immigrant

communities and their descendants. Growing up I also heard "mixed salad," which was the catchphrase of an effort to recognize cultural difference while maintaining the idea that as Americans we are part of one big community together. More recently, "multiculturalism" and "diversity" have become more common as ways of trying to recognize the realities of a country made up of people of different backgrounds and racial and ethnic identities. Even with these developments, though, discussions about assimilation and "cultural fit" continue to loom large in discussions of immigration and Americanness, especially when it comes to communities of color.

For this reason, it's very important for us to think historically, to consider what becoming American has meant in the past and how the basic idea behind the "melting pot" metaphor might still be at work today. When we do, we can see that race has always been a very significant element in the process of becoming American—and what it means to be American in general.

This is the case because people of so many different backgrounds have arrived to the United States over time. But it's also the case because race has been a central feature of being American from the very beginning of the country and continues to play such a significant role in determining to what extent someone is able to live fully as an American.

The idea of whiteness is very important when we think about the process of immigrants and their descendants becoming American. Becoming American for immigrants arriving from Ireland and Southern and Eastern Europe in the nineteenth and early twentieth centuries was made possible by the expansion of what—or who—counted as white over the course of American history. There are a number of scholars whose work can help us think about this process and about how it may, or may not, relate to communities of color in the United States and to race and Americanness more generally.

Historians Mathew Frye Jacobson and Nell Irvin Painter both address the idea that the category of whiteness changed over time to include immigrants from different parts of Europe, making it possible for them to become fully American. Their approaches are a little different, but there are many similarities between their explanations.

Jacobson explores the emergence of the category "Caucasian" during the twentieth century in *Whiteness of a Different Color: European Immigrants and the Alchemy of Race* (Cambridge, MA: Harvard University Press, 1998). The extension of whiteness to include immigrants from Ireland and Southern and Eastern Europe, Jacobson argues, is a case of what he calls "racial alchemy." If we overlook the process by which whiteness in the United States extended beyond its Anglo-Saxon origins, then we allow race to settle into the natural landscape. This makes it difficult to see how race isn't something "natural," but rather something that reflects cultural assumptions and political agendas that are dominant in particular times. Jacobson's argument about the centrality of race in the history of European immigration has significant implications for arguments about assimilation and immigrants of color today.

A central part of Jacobson's argument is that "becoming white" for immigrants from different parts of Europe has often involved people purposefully differentiating themselves from people of color in the United States, especially African Americans. Other scholars make a similar point.

Noel Ignatiev, one of the most widely cited scholars on the history of Irish assimilation into American society, talks about how organizing against African American laborers in nineteenth-century Philadelphia was a crucial part of the process by which Irish immigrants became white in the eyes of other white Americans. Irish communities were also active organizing against Chinese laborers in the Western United States during the same period. For both Jacobson and Ignatiev, whiteness is not a social fact, but rather a political category that people work to gain inclusion into—often by defining themselves against black people. See Ignatiev, *How the Irish Became White* (New York: Routledge, 1995).

According to Nell Irvin Painter's telling in *The History of White People* (New York: W.W. Norton, 2010), there have been several moments over the course of American history that the category of whiteness expanded. The first came with the reduction of property requirements for voting during the early 1800s, opening up full citizenship to poor (male) farmers of Northern European heritage. The second came later in the 1800s and early 1900s, when Irish and German immigrants and their descendants became more fully American in the eyes of Anglo-descended Americans. This second expansion of whiteness came just as immigrants from Southern and Eastern Europe began arriving in greater numbers.

The arrival of these immigrants prompted much discussion about race and cultural fit. Theodore Roosevelt famously adopted the idea that by allowing immigrants from these parts of Europe the United States was committing race suicide because of their inability to assimilate properly. This was an era of continued exclusion of immigrants from Asia, labor unrest (caused in part by the expansion of the labor pool), and the introduction of "Americanization courses" by government and civic organizations. This was also an era that saw the introduction of the idea of "cultural pluralism," which suggested that people from different parts of Europe could retain some elements of their cultural heritage while still becoming white in an American sense.

The third expansion of American whiteness came in the post–World War II era with the massive expansion of the middle class. Thanks to the GI Bill and federal housing subsidies, more recent immigrants from Southern and Eastern Europe began attending universities in much higher numbers and moving to suburbs that were mostly white by design and in practice. The American government actually contributed to divisions between newly incorporated whites and black people by systematically excluding African Americans from the benefits of many federal programs, as it had done during the New Deal.

As Karen Brodkin argues in *How Jews Became White Folks: And What That Says about Race in America* (Philadelphia: Temple University Press, 1998), this was also the era in which Jews became Jewish Americans, partaking in these same government programs in large numbers and joining the growing middle class. For Jewish Americans, however, despite being "model minorities" in many ways, acceptance into "whiteness" was and continues to be tenuous, with anti-Semitism never far from the mind of Jewish communities. Brodkin suggests that this has left Jews in the United States to occupy a position of "not-quite-white."

At this point, I'd like to use an example to explain why a historical perspective on the process of becoming American is so important. People from the Levant, which historically included Syria, Lebanon, and Palestine, began arriving to the United States in the early twentieth century. They were among those whose identities confounded the race-based immigration system in place at the time, leading to court cases trying to adjudicate whether they were white and thus eligible to immigrate.

Today, according to Helen Hatab Samhan, immigrants from this part of the world, who began arriving in greater numbers in the decades after immigration reform in 1965, continue to occupy the position of "not-quite-white." The US government's census categories classify people in these communities, which we now generally call Arab, as white. Yet their everyday experiences, which often reflect how others perceive their identities because of their names, the way they dress, or their appearance, don't necessarily match this designation. See Samhan, "Not Quite White: Race Classification and the Arab-American Experience," in *Arabs in America*, ed. Michael Suleiman (Philadelphia: Temple University Press, 1999), 209–226.

According to Caroline Nagel and Lynn Staeheli, many activists in Arab American communities believe that it's just a matter of time—and a good amount of public outreach—for this to change. Nagel and Staeheli conducted extensive interviews with Arab American activists about the process of becoming American. Many of the people they interviewed consider the Irish an ideal model for becoming American because were able to overcome initial bigotry and discrimination to become part of the American mainstream, all the while celebrating a sense of cultural identity. This is where a historical view on the process of becoming American offers important perspective. See Nagel and Staeheli, "'We're Just Like the Irish': Narratives of Assimilation, Belonging and Citizenship amongst Arab-American Activists," *Citizenship Studies* 9, no. 5 (2005), 485–498.

To continue with the example of Arab Americans, using the Irish model of becoming American introduces some serious complications. Ignatiev (1995) and Painter (2010) argue that an important part of the process by which Irish immigrants and their descendants became white was through active (and often hostile) differentiation from African Americans, thus opening the possibility of identification with white Americans. Given that, as Samhan points out, the experience of many Arab Americans is somewhat akin to the experiences of other communities of color, it's not clear that the path to Americanness through the expansion of whiteness is necessarily open to Arab Americans.

For Nell Irvin Painter, the immigration reform I mentioned earlier, which did away with race-based quotas, significantly transformed the racial landscape of the United States. The Immigration and Nationality Act of 1965 made it possible for people to immigrate to the United States from the Middle East, South Asia, Southeast Asia, and Africa in much greater numbers than ever before. Given these changes, it's not clear whether the integration into American society of immigrants and their descendants from these parts of the world has proceeded and will proceed via the expansion of who counts as white, as in the past.

Thinking about America as a melting pot, which emphasizes assimilation, cultural fit, and the effective expansion of whiteness, doesn't seem to apply today. However uncomfortable it may be, the significant transformation of the demographic and racial landscape in the United States after 1965 is pushing white Americans to reconsider the very notion of becoming American.

This entails doing the hard work of addressing the role of race in Americanness, which requires us to think about the connections between the experiences of African Americans and immigrants from Africa, South Asia, Southeast Asia, and the Middle East, Muslim and otherwise. The ongoing realities of African American racial exclusion from enjoying citizenship in its fullest sense in the United States suggest that other communities of color can't necessarily expect "gradual acceptance" on the same terms as previous generations of immigrants and their descendants.

19 Debates about whether Muslims could ever really be American citizens were part of the country's history from the very beginning. In *Thomas Jefferson's Qur'an: Islam and the Founders* (New York: Vintage, 2014), historian Denise Spellberg describes these debates using records and writings from just before and after independence. It is clear from Spellberg's telling of the story that people debating whether Muslims could ever be fully American did not realize that there were many thousands of Muslims already in the country, nor that there was an intimate connection between Islam and enslaved peoples here. Although we can't ever know precisely the number of enslaved Muslim who were forcibly moved to the United States, records indicate that the number exceeded ten thousand by a significant degree.

CHAPTER 2. REHABILITATION OF PUBLIC HATE

1 *The Extent of Radicalization in the American Muslim Community and That Community's Response: Hearings before the House Committee on Homeland Security*, 112th Congress (2011).

2 Hakimeh Saghaye-Biria offers an overview of the different positions staked out in the March 2011 hearings before the House Committee on Homeland Security. See Saghaye-Biria, "American Muslims as Radicals? A Critical Discourse Analysis of the US Congressional Hearing on 'The Extent of Radicalization in the American Muslim Community and That Community's Response,'" *Discourse & Society* 23, no. 5 (2012), 508–524, DOI: 10.1 177/0957926512452972

3 Speaking just after September 11, President George W. Bush gave prepared remarks declaring Islam to be a religion of peace and Muslims to be important contributors to American society. Bush, "'Islam Is Peace,' Says President," Washington, DC, Islamic Center of Washington, DC, September 17, 2001, https://georgewbush-whitehouse.archives.gov.

4 "Time Poll Results: Americans' Views on the Campaign, Religion and the Mosque Controversy," *Time*, last modified August 18, 2010, http://content.time.com.

5 Jeanne Halgren Kilde argues that the Park51 controversy, and especially the presentation of Ground Zero as sacred space, led many Americans who otherwise support religious liberty to oppose the construction of a Muslim community center in lower Manhattan. The increasing influence of anti-Muslim sentiment in the wake of the controversy, she says, evidences "a deep ambivalence regarding the legitimate civic membership of Muslim Americans." This is precisely the ambivalence I described in connection to public hate in the introduction. See Kilde, "The Park 51/Ground Zero Mosque Controversy and Sacred Sites as Contested Space," *Religions* (2011), 297–311, DOI: 10.3390/ rel2030297.

6 In a note in chapter 1, I talk about the work of Noel Ignatiev (1995) on the process by which Irish immigrants and their descendants became American. He argues that Irish efforts to distinguish themselves from African Americans were a significant part of this process, especially in the context of Philadelphia, where riots, often but not always related to labor disputes, were a regular feature of city life. Race played a significant role in a good number of these riots. Analyzing particular riots in the second half of the nineteenth century in which mobs, which included members of Irish communities, targeted African Americans, Ignatiev says,

> We begin with the knowledge that some Irish had reasons to hate and fear people of black skin. We assume that not all Irish felt that way, at any rate not strongly enough to join a white supremacist mob; this we know from our general knowledge of humanity, of Irish history, and, most of all, from the fact that the mob numbered only hundreds in a community of many thousand. Yet that organized force of hundreds was able to batter those who opposed it, or even those who held back, into silence and submission, so that in time it came to speak for the entire community. Rioters do not merely reflect public opinion; they shape it.

> Today, riots are a less common feature of public life in the United States. But Ignatiev's analysis is significant for us because it remains true that a limited number of people, who do not necessarily represent the public at large, can shape public opinion in very dangerous ways. Anti-Muslim activists and anti-Muslim public officials play this role today when it comes to fomenting suspicion and hatred of Muslims.

CHAPTER 3. POLICING MUSLIM PUBLIC LIFE

1 Lawyer and First Amendment advocate Asma Uddin has been tracking the argument that Islam is a political ideology and not a religion over the past decade as it has become a more common

feature of anti-Muslim discourse. The effort to block mosque construction in Murfreesboro in 2010 was the first instance, but since then many public figures, including state legislators across the country as well as high-level federal political appointees, have declared that Islam is in fact a political ideology and not a religion. This argument has the potential to influence public policy affecting a vast range of elements of public life for Muslims, from land use and the creation of legal documents like wills to curriculums in public schools and the rights of incarcerated individuals. Uddin argues that efforts to discredit Islam as a religion constitute a threat to religious liberty in general. See Uddin, *When Islam Is Not a Religion: Inside America's Fight for Religious Liberty* (New York: Pegasus Books, 2019). You can find shorter treatments of her argument in two pieces available online: Uddin, "The Latest Attack on Islam: It's Not a Religion," *New York Times*, September 26, 2018, www.nytimes.com; and Simran Jeet Singh, "Asma Uddin: If We Deprive Islam of Its Status as a Religion, All Religion Is Threatened," *Religion News Service*, April 30, 2019, https://religion-news.com.

2 Just because someone doesn't directly experience violence doesn't mean that it won't have a profound effect on them. Here, as in other parts of this book, drawing on the experience of African American communities can offer very important insights.

In *Hanging Bridge: Racial Violence and America's Civil Rights Century* (New York: Oxford University Press, 2016), Jason Ward uses a bridge that served as a lynching site as a window into a broader story, delving into the history of Clarke County, Mississippi, to explore the relationship between racial violence and subtler forms of oppression during the nineteenth and twentieth centuries. "White supremacists," he writes, "understood that violence served a higher purpose than punishing individuals," especially at times when people feel like an "existing order" is somehow under attack.

Ward shows that racial violence, while often targeting individuals, serves what I'll call a "pedagogical purpose" in relation to larger groups. It's meant to scare, intimidate, and terrorize, preventing groups of people from feeling as if they belong in public space. To be clear, I am not equating the horror of systematic lynchings against African Americans with forms of violence other communities of color experience. I am suggesting that we can take from this history a very important point—that people don't need to experience violence directly for it to leave a deep mark, especially regarding belonging.

3 Sara Ahmed (2001) calls for a reorientation of how we think about hate crimes in "The Organization of Hate," cited in a note to the introduction—to focus more on the effect of an incident rather than the motivation.

Ahmed writes, "Hate may respond to the particular, but it tends to do so by aligning the particular with the general; 'I hate you because you are this or that,' where the 'this' or 'that' evokes a group that the individual comes to *stand for* or *stand in for*." The connection between an individual object of hate and a larger group they stand in for is precisely what makes a crime targeting someone for who they are (or are perceived to be) a hate crime. "[H]ate crime works as a form of violence against groups *through* violence against the bodies of individuals."

As I read Ahmed, I was reminded of a story I read in the *Burlington Free Press* about hate crimes or, more specifically, how law enforcement officials decide whether something constitutes a hate crime. (Elizabeth Murray, "Hate Crimes in Vermont: Why Police, Lawyers Sometimes Disagree if Someone Crossed the Line," *Burlington Free Press*, October 10, 2018.) The determination about adding hate-crime enhancements to a given offense often rests on the extent to which officials can clearly identify hate as a motivating factor in the commission of a crime. This approach certainly opens up questions about how the law defines hate and distinguishes it, for example, from constitutionally protected speech.

But it seems just as important to ask how the focus on the motivation of the perpetrator affects our ability to determine whether something someone said or did constitutes a hate crime. Shifting away from motivation, or at least balancing motivation with the *effects* of a given incident, would likely fundamentally change the way that law enforcement officials determine whether something falls under a hate-crime statute.

Shifting away from a focus on motivation to at least include consideration of effects also helps us think about the relationship between hate crimes and activities and behaviors that don't rise to the level of punishable offenses. The kinds of everyday indignities that mark the experiences of many communities (especially communities of color) in the United States then become something much more serious than "uncomfortable" episodes. People outside of those communities may come to see everyday indignities as the backdrop of life itself and part of the process through which people become individuals, and as individuals part of (or not part of) our public life.

4 Another essay from the excellent volume I mentioned in a previous note, *Fear: Critical Geopolitics and Everyday Life*, offers important insight on the kinds of experiences that affect peoples' understandings of belonging.

Michael Haldrup, Lasse Koefoed, and Kirsten Simonsen remind us that the maintenance of community boundaries, who's in and who's out, who belongs and who doesn't, occurs in often very subtle, everyday ways that don't rise to the level of hate crimes and even behavior that most people would recognize as excluding others. They emphasize the place of passions and emotions, such as love, desire, hate, fear, anxiety, or aggression, in guiding how we relate to others and the way that this in turn affects how our interactions unfold and our social worlds develop over time. See

Haldrup, Koefoed, and Simonsen, "Practising Fear: Encountering O/other Bodies," in *Fear: Critical Geopolitics and Everyday Life*, ed. Rachel Pain and Susan Smith (London: Ashgate, 2008), 117–128.

General social, cultural, and political discourses about others are certainly part of the picture, but Haldrup, Koefoed, and Simonsen want us to consider how actual encounters with actual bodies, especially in public spaces, also contribute to how we interact with the world around us. The authors begin by discussing the role of language in everyday encounters, especially regarding national identity. "Everyday practices," they write, "reproduce [singular] national identity in ways so ordinary, so commonplace, that they escape attention altogether. It can be in speech through routinely and unconsciously using homeland-making phrases; small unnoticed words such as 'we,' 'the' people, 'this' country, 'here,' 'society.'"

But language is not the only way we communicate things. How we engage with people, or don't engage with them, in shared public space also sends important cues. We can make these decisions based on how people look, the color of their skin, what they're wearing, or how they speak. "Familiar bodies can be incorporated through a sense of community, being with each other as like bodies, while strange bodies more likely are expelled from bodily space and moved apart as different bodies." The idea of incorporating or expelling people from our own slice of shared public space based on how we perceive them and relate to them illustrates how little decisions can communicate a lot about how we feel about others.

The way we go about incorporating or expelling others from our slice of shared public space can be more or less warm or aggressive. Whatever the case, our encounters with difference will always flow from our emotions and will produce some kind of emotional response (in both ourselves and those with whom we share an encounter, however brief). These are the moments through which our social worlds are built.

Importantly, all of our encounters occur in light of our relative social status among others. Not everyone has the power in public space to welcome or exclude others. This very idea depends on the notion that you feel like you belong in public space. Our social worlds are deeply tied to our relationship to public space.

5 In this particular case, the grocery store served as what scholar Helga Leitner calls a space of encounter. See Leitner, "Spaces of Encounter: Immigration, Race, Class, and the Politics of Belonging in Small-Town America," *Annals of the Association of American Geographers* 102, no. 4 (2012), 828–846.

Spaces of encounter are those spaces in which people of different races, religions, and backgrounds come together as they move through their everyday lives. Spaces of encounter are most often public, and thus provide an opportunity to consider the connections between public space, citizenship, and the politics of belonging.

Dearborn is a city with significant Arab and Arabic-speaking communities, who began arriving in the early twentieth century. Census data suggests that the city is 89 percent white, but we know that racial classification is a very complicated business and that census categories don't necessarily match how people think of themselves and how others treat them based on their appearance. Many of those in this census category descend from European immigrants, while many others descend from the Middle East. The incident in the grocery store reflects the particular histories and complexities of life in Dearborn, but spaces of encounter are not limited to urbanized areas with very diverse populations. In fact, Leitner's work explores the concept of spaces of encounter in small-town America.

Leitner draws from her focus-group interviews in a rural Minnesota town to consider the relationship between place and the politics of belonging. She found that how people understand place—whether a local downtown, a region, or a country—is deeply connected to racialization, or the process of ascribing "physical and cultural differences to individuals and groups." The reality of this deep interconnection between place and racialization play out in what Leitner calls "spaces of encounters." The small city in which she conducted field work is just such a space.

Encounters, Leitner argues, are not just about face-to-face contact. Each instance of face-to-face contact calls forth histories and connections that provide meaning to the encounter. "Towns, regions, and nation-states become conjoined with particular national and cultural identities—such as the rural Midwest with heartland of white America—identities that are challenged by the entry and presence of migrants regarded as culturally and racially different."

Of course, face-to-face encounters do occur in intimate settings of local life, where the realities of larger histories and cultural identities play out in real time. Cultural identities, Leitner points out, "are also made in the *everyday spaces* (supermarkets, houses of worship, residential neighborhoods, factory floors, public space) where they undergo racial encoding." Racialization, in other words, is very much connected to large stories about national or regional identity, but often plays and takes on concrete meaning in the spaces of everyday lives.

For many residents of the small city in which Leitner interviewed people, their community was, and in many ways still is, characterized by its whiteness, both in terms of the appearance of "real" residents and their perceived cultural attributes. Other residents, who tended to have higher degrees of educational attainment and to be part of local economic elites, acknowledged the changes that were unfolding around them and considered it their responsibility to help new arrivals acculturate. Despite a difference in the language they used to describe immigrant communities of color, Leitner saw some striking similarities.

Leitner talks about being struck by the extent to which participants in focus groups focused on their sense of difference from immigrant communities in the city. She paraphrases what she heard: "They are not like us, in terms of their culture, behavior, bodily appearance, and language." *They* are, in other words, fundamentally out of place, a relationship to the city that can change only insofar as they become more like white residents.

The politics of belonging on display in these interviews, according to Leitner, is predicated almost entirely on assimilationist understandings of being/becoming American. "For the majority of white residents, belonging is conditional on immigrants becoming like them, through expectations that immigrants adapt to prevailing norms and culture. Drawing on assimilationist imaginary, belonging requires conformity with white American values and norms—explicit norms that are simultaneously unmarked, ordinary, and taken for granted." American culture, in other words, has fairly well-defined and closed boundaries, and acting within them is what ensures that someone belongs, or ceases to be out of place.

6 Saher Selod devotes an entire chapter of her book, *Forever Suspect* (2018), to experiences related to travel. Selod interviewed a large and diverse collection of participants for her study. She found some common themes, including that Muslim travelers experience uncommonly high incidences of random searches while moving through security. She also found that experiences of airport security are gendered, with men tending to encounter challenges relating to being on a no-fly list of some kind and women tending to be pulled aside for screening at very high rates. This is especially true for women who wear head coverings of some kind.

The very public spectacle of being pulled aside or questioned extensively in front of other passengers is part of what Selod calls "performing security." This is less about protecting people, she argues, than it is about easing people's fears—that is, easing the fears of non-Muslim passengers at the expense of Muslims and others who security agents identify as (or assume to be) Muslim.

Of course, the experience of flying while Muslim isn't just about encounters with airport security. Interactions with other passengers can be just as troubling.

7   In a note earlier in this chapter, I talk about Sara Ahmed's point about shifting perspectives on hate crimes from the motivation of the assailant to the experience of the target. Changing how we frame hate crimes makes it possible for us to more effectively consider how a spectrum of experiences, only some of which arise from being a target of criminal activity, affects people over time.

8   As I've been arguing throughout this book, wondering if, or when, something serious will happen to you when you leave your home has significant implications for how you feel about public space. This, in turn, has big implications for our ability to fully engage in public life to the fullest extent we desire.

Human, cultural, and social geographers, especially those working on questions relating to citizenship, are very interested in what kinds of things affect people's ability to move in and around public space. These can be official policies relating to mobility—things like passports and border controls. But there are many other, less formal things that affect people's movement in and out of public space, often connected to everyday interactions with other people.

In the United States, everyday experiences that affect people's ability to be in shared or public space—safely and comfortably—often have to do with race, as I discussed in chapter 1.

Increasingly, scholars are looking at how Islam and Muslims have become "racialized" in the United States, a development that has led to the kind of experiences that Tahera had on the airplane. The accumulation of such experiences can build over time to make people feel unsafe and thus unable to move freely in shared, public space.

Writing in a collection that I've talked about in other notes, Peter Hopkins and Susan Smith draw on interviews with young adult Muslims in Scotland to explore fear in the age of the war on terror. See Hopkins and Smith, "Scaling Segregation; Racialising Fear," in Pain and Smith, *Fear*, 104–116. Although their interview subjects don't live in the United States, Hopkins and Smith offer insights that apply equally well to our own society.

They suggest that in the age of the War on Terror, what had been a positive development in many Western societies—the recognition and celebration of difference—has become the basis of new arguments about the incompatibility of Muslims and Western societies. "We are concerned with the elision of race and religion which . . . reassert[s] a divide between the West and the Rest." The racialization of Muslims as fundamentally Other has had tremendous consequences for the everyday lives of Muslims for whom Western societies are home.

Fear and managing perceived risks associated with the Other have long been the basis of efforts to manage access to space and territory, whether neighborhoods, nation-states, or empires. Race has played a huge role in political decision-making around such efforts. Religion has of late become an equally significant marker of difference, with race and religion becoming increasingly conflated when it comes to security.

Yet focusing on policies and official procedures around managing space makes it difficult to see how the everyday behaviors of some, especially those with relatively high social status, can affect how others perceive how welcome they are in a given space. The same attitudes at work in policies and procedures meant to keep certain groups from accessing particular spaces or territories show themselves in everyday encounters and interactions.

Looking a certain way or wearing particular kinds of clothing that non-Muslims might associate with Islam, for example, can elicit rude or insulting behavior, harassments, threats, or even violence. These possibilities affect the way that people think about what space they can occupy and how they can occupy it. "It is the prospect of any encounter turning sour—the constant threat of violence simply because of some combination of location and appearance—that makes fear so powerful an impulse to separation." Hopkins and Smith are careful to point out that the lives of all Muslims aren't entirely beset by fear. But based on their fieldwork and interviews with young adult Muslims in Scotland, they argue that their lives are marked by a low-level anxiety.

Low-level anxiety, a nagging sense that things *could* go quite wrong, can lead to a withdrawal from public space and a retreat to spaces in which one feels a general sense of being welcome, a kind of self-segregation. Low-level anxiety can also lead to efforts to maintain invisibility in public, shared space. Being invisible might entail removing markers of difference—dressing like others, speaking like others, or going by a name that is less obviously associated with being Muslim. Both responses to low-level anxiety are about minimizing risk.

Many of the people Hopkins and Smith interviewed talked about a kind of conditional belonging, where even if they were born in Scotland they need to act and appear a certain way to minimize risk. This often includes making sure to distance the local community from broader discourses around the incompatibility of Muslims and Western societies—the real problem is "out there," not right where people live.

The very fact that low-level anxiety is such an ever-present part of their lives, though, would seem to suggest that experiences of exclusion on the basis of particular racialized markers are in fact the result of attitudes and accompanying behaviors in local communities. Focusing on official policies and procedures meant to manage access to particular spaces, such as travel bans, can make it difficult to see how everyday experiences can affect access to space in powerful ways.

9 Juliane Hammer (2019) argues that the threat of Muslim reproduction is a central feature of contemporary anti-Muslim hostility. She cites King's comments as well as those of Representative Louis Gohmert of Texas, who in 2010 claimed (without evidence) on the House floor that foreign Muslim women were coming to the United States, having babies (who are US citizens), and then returning home to raise "terror babies." Megan Goodwin calls concerns about the threat posed by "foreign babies" and Muslim reproduction, including Muslim men marrying white women, "contraceptive nationalism." See Goodwin, "'They Do That to Foreign Women': Domestic Terrorism and Contraceptive Nationalism in *Not Without My Daughter*," *Muslim World* 106 (2016), 759–780.

CHAPTER 4. PUBLIC AFTERMATHS OF SEPTEMBER 11

1 Lara Engel and Adam Smidi argue that *affect* is a crucial concept for understanding the connection between September 11 and contemporary anti-Muslim hostility. They analyze "the impact of post-9/11 anxiety, anger, and fear on affective resonance, the degree to which the impact of the events of September 11, 2001, has continued to intensify and amplify the circulation of affect across communities." It's these lasting repercussions, they suggest, that make fear-based, and typically untruthful, claims by anti-Muslim activists so successful in generating anti-Muslim sentiment. See Engel and Smidi, "How Affect Overrides Fact:

Anti-Muslim Politicized Rhetoric in the Post-Truth Era," in *Affect, Emotion, and Rhetorical Persuasions in Mass Communication*, ed. Lei Zhang and Carlton Clark (New York: Routledge, 2018), 115–129. The concept of affect connects back to a note from the introduction about Sara Ahmed's exploration of hate. She argues that emotion isn't just something we understand cognitively (I understand that I feel a certain way, for example). Emotion operates at an often-unconscious level to profoundly affect how we understand everything around us, how we interact with others—in short, how we act in the world. Donovan Schaefer explores the connection between affect and Islamophobia in *Religious Affects* (Durham, NC: Duke University Press, 2015).

2 The Global Terrorism Database, housed at the University of Maryland, is a project of the National Consortium for the Study of Terrorism and Responses to Terrorism. You can find the database at www.start.umd.edu/gtd.

3 The complete results of the study are in Erin Kearns, Allison Betus, and Anthony Lemiuex, "Why Do Some Terrorist Attacks Receive More Media Attention than Others?," *Justice Quarterly* (2018), DOI: 10.1080/07418825.2018.1524507. You can find an accessible analysis of the study results in an article by Mona Chalabi, "Terror Attacks by Muslims Receive 357% More Press Attention, Study Finds," *Guardian*, July 20, 2018, www.theguardian.com.

4 Scholars began writing about the idea of cultural trauma as a social, rather than psychological, phenomenon in the early 2000s, in an effort to understand the broad effects of a shocking development that changes the lives of people far beyond those directly involved. A significant contribution to the development of this area of thought is *Cultural Trauma and Collective Identity*, co-authored by Jeffrey Alexander, Ron Eyerman, Bernard Giesen, Neil Smelser, and Piotr Sztompka (Berkeley: University of

California Press, 2004). The book's epilogue, written by Smelser, specifically discusses the September 11 attacks as creating significant cultural trauma in the United States.

5 Historian Sylvester Johnson makes this point in "'True Faith and Allegiance'—Religion and the FBI," the introduction to *The FBI and Religion: Faith and National Security before and after 9/11* (Berkeley: University of California Press, 2017). Beyond Johnson's work, this book has essays from a number of different scholars. Of particular interest may be Michael Barkun's "The FBI and American Muslims after 9/11."

6 In 2012, Matt Apuzzo, Adam Goldman, Eileen Sullivan, and Chris Hawley won a Pulitzer Prize for their reporting in the *New York Times* about the NYPD's surveillance of Muslim communities in and around New York City. Apuzzo and Goldman then wrote *Enemies Within: Inside the NYPD's Secret Spying Unit and bin Laden's Final Plot against America* (New York: Touchstone, 2013).

7 Evelyn Alsultany devotes an entire chapter of her book *Arabs and Muslims in the Media: Race and Representation after 9/11* (New York: NYU Press, 2012) to how these tensions played out in popular culture in the years following September 11, 2001. What I appreciate about Alsultany's work is that she digs deep into episodes of shows, especially dramas involving crimes, law enforcement, and the legal system, that were popular at that time. These include *The Practice*, *NYPD Blue*, and *Law and Order*. This approach builds a vivid picture of what lots of people were watching, capturing the moment in a compelling manner.

She argues that television shows like these, meant for mass consumption, often engage contemporary issues in a way that will appeal to as broad an audience as possible—trying, in the process, to balance different perspectives on hot-button issues. What she noticed in analyzing episodes of these shows involving Arabs and Muslims in the months and years following September 11 is that many of them were pretty sympathetic. Using a variety of scenarios, including hate crimes or false accusations against Arabs and Muslims, they echoed what people were hearing from the Bush administration and other political leaders: American Muslims were not responsible for the actions of a few people who had hijacked an honorable religion for their own violent ends. Yet these episodes rarely left things at that.

The episodes that Alsultany analyzes often conclude with scenes that try to make the audience feel a little bit better about the injustice that they have just watched unfold. They might portray unfounded suspicion or false accusations of terrorist activity as understandable given the circumstances—unfortunate, but understandable. Or, similarly, they might portray a hate crime against an Arab or Muslim as exceptions born of an exceptional moment in the country's history.

In these tellings, things will eventually return to normal. We won't live in a state of exception forever. We'll neutralize the threat of Islamic terrorism, rendering racial profiling unnecessary. A norm of racial equality will eventually overcome bigotry, guiding American society beyond hate crimes against people and communities of color.

Reassurances may be an essential feature of good TV drama (and a reflection of our hopes), but the reality of anti-Muslim hostility is much more complex in post-9/11 American life. Ambivalence around the rights and full citizenship of American Muslims became a more visible part of public discourse in the months and years after the September 11 attacks. The suspicion of Muslims that makes the suspension of full citizenship appear a reasonable step to take, however, has much deeper cultural and emotional roots.

Among the most creative attempts to shed light on just how ingrained negative stereotypes about Muslims are in American culture is Peter Gottschalk and Gabriel Greenberg's *Islamophobia: Making Muslims the Enemy* (2d ed.; Lanham, MD: Rowman &

Littlefield, 2018). They suggest that analyzing political cartoons is a good way of looking at anti-Muslim hostility in the months and years after September 11 because they are immediate responses to unfolding events, often reflecting something much rawer than a finely tuned TV drama or film.

Political cartoons, which seek to convey a lot of information in a little space with minimal text, often depend on symbols and existing associations to convey a meaning beyond the lines drawn on the page (or screen). In the months and years immediately following September 11, cartoons often used swords, mosques, veiled women, camels, and angry or confused men in turbans or some kind of head covering to represent Muslims. These symbols draw on centuries-old stereotypes about Islam and Muslim societies that have long been part of American popular culture, updating them to comment on current affairs.

The stereotypes these symbols represent reinforce the idea that Muslims are fundamentally different from "us." They are hapless, deceitful, oppressive, violent, evil, overly religious (or the wrong kind of religious), and anti-modern. At the time, many Americans were asking why people would carry out such horrific atrocities. The cartoons that Gottschalk and Greenberg analyze give ready answers.

More than that, though, political cartoons create an often-implicit impression of what Americans are through negative association. They (Muslims) hate us because we are not like them. We are resolute, honest, freedom loving, reluctantly at war, a force for good, appropriately religious, and thoroughly modern. We are, in other very simple terms, good.

In *Muslims in the Western Imagination*, Sophia Rose Arjana ties post–September 11 depictions to long histories of Western representations that have presented Muslims as monsters, from demons and giants in the Middle Ages to zombies in more contemporary times. Depicting Muslims as monsters, she argues, has made it possible to dehumanize Muslims and to present all Muslims in terms of threatening stereotypes, most recently as terrorists, on TV, in movies, and in political cartoons. See Arjana, *Muslims in the Western Imagination* (Oxford: Oxford University Press, 2015).

8 In previous notes, I have drawn on the work of Jason Ward (2016) and Sara Ahmed (2001) to talk about the idea of the "pedagogical purpose" of violence targeting individuals in vulnerable groups. The effect of such violence is not limited to the individual who has been targeted; incidents send a message to others in the same communities that they aren't welcome, that they don't belong. News of such attacks can move through social networks, social media, and local and national media, reaching people with no direct connection to those targeted.

9 Leila Fadl, "Coping with the Persistent Trauma of Anti-Muslim Rhetoric and Violence," *NPR*, March 19, 2019, www.npr.org.

10 Bryan D. Byers and James A. Jones, "The Impact of the Terrorist Attacks of 9/11 on Anti-Islamic Hate Crime," *Journal of Ethnicity in Criminal Justice* 5, no. 1 (2007), 43–56.

CHAPTER 5. HUMANIZING PUBLIC LIFE

1 You can watch video of the exchange at "Opponent at the Islamic Center Meeting," *Free Lance–Star*, November 19, 2015, www.fredericksburg.com.

2 National advocacy organizations have been another important source of humanizing efforts in recent years. One such organization is the Council on American Islamic Relations, or CAIR. A favorite target of suspicion for contemporary anti-Muslim activists, CAIR was founded in 1994 to counter negative stereotypes about Islam, especially in media. The organization has redoubled its efforts in the post–September 11 era. It has also become more active in providing legal support to Muslims who have been targets of anti-Muslim activity as well as building coalitions with other communities around civil rights in the United States.

Muslim Advocates is another national advocacy organization that has risen to prominence in the post–September 11 era. The core of its mission is legal support.

Organizations like CAIR and Muslim Advocates do important work supporting Muslim communities and building alliances with other vulnerable groups. The Mapping Islamophobia dataset includes some instances of larger organizations like these engaging in humanizing outreach, especially if local chapters are involved.

There are also organizations that focus on provide educational services, including training for intergroup dialogue, seminars on cultural diversity for corporations and public institutions, and curriculums relating to public outreach. One example of this kind of organization is the Islamic Groups Network (ING). ING, based in Northern California, was founded in 1993 and describes itself as working within a First Amendment framework of religious freedom and pluralism to promote tolerance and understanding.

Other organizations work at a more local level but have begun to establish a national presence in recognition of those efforts. The Muslim Anti-Racism Collaborative (MuslimARC), based in Detroit, focuses on educating Muslims about the nature of racisms and how they create social disparities, especially for communities of color. MuslimARC describes itself as a human rights education organization. It is similar to the Inner-City Muslim Action Network in Chicago, which works at a more local level to support the needs of Muslim and other communities.

When my students and I are gathering data, we try to focus especially on individuals and local communities doing humanizing work. This includes the work of Muslim scholar-activists when appropriate. Sometimes the boundaries between advocacy organizations, local communities, and individuals can be blurry. That said, the vast majority of our data reflects the work of everyday people who take time out of their busy lives to demonstrate their humanity to others.

3 Todd Green provides an extended discussion of collective guilt in *Presumed Guilty: Why We Shouldn't Ask Muslims to Condemn Terrorism* (Minneapolis: Fortress Press, 2018).

4 Zain Abdullah, "American Muslims in the Contemporary World," in *The Cambridge Companion to American Islam*, ed. Juliane Hammer and Omid Safi (New York: Cambridge University Press), 65–82.

CONCLUSION

1 Maheen Haq. Interview by Caleb Elfenbein. Grinnell, Iowa, and Hagerstown, Maryland, May 29, 2019.

INDEX

Abu-Salha, Razan Mohammad, 77
Abu-Salha, Yusor Mohammad, 77
ACT for America, 44
activism: anti-Muslim, 5, 35–37, 47–52, 54,
  58–59, 87, 91; anti-shari'a, 43–44; by
  Geller, 39–40, 43, 47
activity, anti-Muslim. *See* anti-Muslim
  activity
Afghanistan, 105
African Americans, 17, 28, 188n18; history
  of, 23–24; incarceration of, 166n2;
  Irish targeting, 196n6; Muslim, 19, 24,
  101, 180n14; public space and, 26–27,
  183n16, 188n17; violence toward, 197n2
Afzaal, Hadiya, 141
Agema, David, 46
Ahmad, Jalaluddin, 131
Ahmad, Tahera, 78, 204n8
Ahmed, Sara, 169n3, 198n3, 204n7, 207n1,
  212n8
airport security, 78, 203n6
Akhtar, Pervaz, 38
ALAC. *See* American Laws for American
  Courts
Alexander, Jeffrey, 208n4
Ali, Wajahat, 141
allyship, 144, 145–46, 151; by non-Muslims,
  127, 143, 147
al-Qa'ida, 32, 57, 105
Alryyes, Ala, 179n13
Alsultany, Evelyn, 209n7
American Center for Law and Justice, 48
American Freedom Defense Initiative, 59
American Laws for American Courts
  (ALAC), 44–47, 72–74, 93

"American Muslims as Radicals?"
  (Saghaye-Biria), 195n2
anger, and hate, 169n3
"anti-indoctrination" bill, 74
anti-mosque campaigns, 72
anti-Muslim activity, 5–6, 75–80, 117,
  166n2; documenting, 87; humanization
  work in response to, 122, 123–24, 127,
  128; Mapping Islamophobia database
  and, 162n2; Park51 project leading
  to, 48–55, 71; terrorist attacks leading to, 130–31; after Trump election,
  69. *See also* anti-Muslim hate crimes;
  anti-Muslim hostility; anti-Muslim
  sentiment
anti-Muslim hate crimes, 30, 77, 87, 114,
  166n2, 174n3; decrease in, 115; emotions and, 199n4; as hoaxes, 162n3;
  humanization in response to, 127–28;
  after September 11, 97, 110–12; thinking
  about, 198n3, 204n7
anti-Muslim hostility, 11, 23, 24, 29–31,
  159n1, 183n16; public life and, 26–27,
  48, 66, 69; after September 11, 97, 116;
  skepticism of, 162n3; Trump and,
  67–69
anti-Muslim legislation, 31, 48, 74–75;
  ALAC-based, 44–47, 72–73, 93; anti-
  shari'a, 45, 46, 53, 70, 73; Tennessee
  Religious Freedom Act (2009), 71
anti-Muslim sentiment, 2, 4, 5, 67; collective guilt and, 129; humanization
  as a response to, 122, 123–24, 127, 128;
  radicalization and, 32; after September
  11 2001, 34–35, 129, 209n7

ABOUT THE AUTHOR

Caleb Elfenbein is Associate Professor in the Departments of History and Religious Studies at Grinnell College, where he is also Director of the Center for the Humanities. His work explores religion, community, public life, and human welfare in different times and places.

NORTH AMERICAN RELIGIONS

Series Editors: Tracy Fessenden (Religious Studies, Arizona State University), Laura Levitt (Religious Studies, Temple University), and David Harrington Watt (History, Haverford College)

In recent years a cadre of industrious, imaginative, and theoretically sophisticated scholars of religion have focused their attention on North America. As a result, the field is far more subtle, expansive, and interdisciplinary than it was just two decades ago. The North American Religions series builds on this transformative momentum. Books in the series move among the discourses of ethnography, cultural analysis, and historical study to shed new light on a wide range of religious experiences, practices, and institutions. They explore topics such as lived religion, popular religious movements, religion and social power, religion and cultural reproduction, and the relationship between secular and religious institutions and practices. The series focuses primarily, but not exclusively, on religion in the United States in the twentieth and twenty-first centuries.

Books in the series:

Ava Chamberlain, *The Notorious Elizabeth Tuttle: Marriage, Murder, and Madness in the Family of Jonathan Edwards*

Terry Rey and Alex Stepick, *Crossing the Water and Keeping the Faith: Haitian Religion in Miami*

Jodi Eichler-Levine, *Suffer the Little Children: Uses of the Past in Jewish and African American Children's Literature*

Isaac Weiner, *Religion Out Loud: Religious Sound, Public Space, and American Pluralism*

Hillary Kaell, *Walking Where Jesus Walked: American Christians and Holy Land Pilgrimage*

Brett Hendrickson, *Border Medicine: A Transcultural History of Mexican American Curanderismo*

Annie Blazer, *Playing for God: Evangelical Women and the Unintended Consequences of Sports Ministry*

Elizabeth Pérez, *Religion in the Kitchen: Cooking, Talking, and the Making of Black Atlantic Traditions*

Kerry Mitchell, *Spirituality and the State: Managing Nature and Experience in America's National Parks*

Finbarr Curtis, *The Production of American Religious Freedom*

M. Cooper Harriss, *Ralph Ellison's Invisible Theology*

Shari Rabin, *Jews on the Frontier: Religion and Mobility in Nineteenth-Century America*

Ari Y. Kelman, *Shout to the Lord: Making Worship Music in Evangelical America*

Joshua Dubler and Isaac Weiner, *Religion, Law, USA*

Elizabeth Fenton, *Old Canaan in a New World: Native Americans and the Lost Tribes of Israel*

Alyssa Maldonado-Estrada, *Lifeblood of the Parish: Masculinity and Catholic Devotion in Williamsburg, Brooklyn*

Caleb Iyer Elfenbein, *Fear in Our Hearts: What Islamophobia Tells Us about America*